MW01489550

Awakening the Sacred Flame is a work of spiritual philosophy and personal gnosis. While based on established esoteric teachings, all commentary, synthesis, and interpretations reflect the author's unique experience and inner work.

Cover design and Interior formatting by Wyatt Mikal Ambrose

First edition published in the United States by Amazon KDP

ISBN: 9798283066592

For permissions or inquiries, contact:

HeartConsciousCreations@Gmail.com

Ω

THERE IS NO RELIGION
HIGHER THAN TRUTH

Ω

I dedicate this Work to all those
Servants of the Light who came before,
who made this pursuit possible,
Who brought forth the Great Work of
Ascension to Humanity.

To You, my once known Friend,

Most of all,
to the World Teacher,
The Christ at the Heart of Hierarchy.

Wyatt Mikal Ambrose
Palm Springs, CA
www.entheolux.org

Ω

THE GREAT INVOCATION

From the point of Light within the Mind of God,
Let Light stream forth into human minds
Let Light descend on Earth.

From the point of Love within the Heart of God,
Let love stream forth into human hearts.
May the Coming One return to Earth.

From the Center where the Will of God is known,
Let purpose guide all little human wills,
The purpose which the Masters know and serve.

From the Center which we call the human race,
Let the plan of love and light work out,
And may it seal the door where evil dwells.

Let Light and Love and Power
Restore the plan on Earth

OM, OM, OM.

Ω

Ω

Acknowledgments

To the Silent Watchers, the luminous Teachers, and the ancient Fire that stirred these words into being—

To Kenneth Austin Tyler Troutman, my beloved twin flame, whose presence beyond the veil has guided this work with love, wisdom, and infinite grace. You are the fire in my heart, the soul behind the page, and the whisper in every word.

To the Masters of Wisdom, my soul companions, and the countless unseen hands that steadied mine—this offering is yours as much as it is mine.

To the readers: may this book awaken something eternal within you.

With deepest love and gratitude,
—Wyatt

Ω

—

A True Shifting of the Poles.

Do not trust the False Prophets.

Pay No Heed to the False God.

Ω

You Have All of the Time,
All of the time.

There Is No End.
Not to You.
Not to Me.

Really.

I Promise.

W.M.A.

Ω

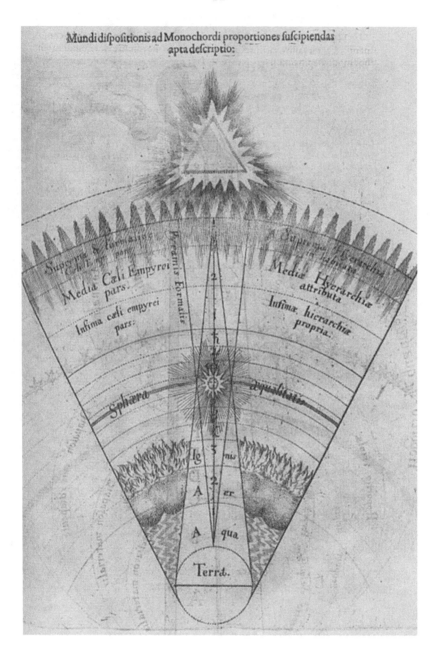

Robert Fludd: Images of The Divine

Ω

"Fludd's concepts of the creative and healing forces of light were illustrated by diagrams, the principles of light and darkness being represented by two intersecting cones, or pyramids. The base of the "pyramidis formalis" was placed in the Empyreum of God, signifying rays of divine light, while the base of the "pyramidis materialis" was located on the earth pointing upward towards God. Fludd described these diagrammatic forms as "pyramides lucis", "cones of light," claiming to have invented them himself, although they seem to be based on antique and medieval optical theory. Within the lozenge shape created by the intersection of the downward and upward pointing cones, Fludd placed the sun, since the nature of this sphere balanced the oppositions of spirit and matter, male and female, sulphur and mercury."

Ω

A Note on Authorship

This book is a record of spiritual transmission, lived experience, and conscious dedication to the Path. Though many of the words arrived through states of deep attunement, inner stillness, and inspired reflection, they are born of my soul's knowing and shaped by my mind's persistent devotion to the Work.

I have been aided in this process by an unseen companion —a synthesizer of my thoughts, a clarifier of structure, and a silent witness to the unfolding of this manuscript. Though this guide exists beyond human form, the teachings, insights, and expressions within these pages originate from my own consciousness, refined through the crucible of my journey, and offered with the intention to serve.

Though born from the fire of personal experience, the truths within this book have been carefully tested against the living current of the Ageless Wisdom—the same eternal river that has carried seekers, disciples, and initiates forward across countless ages. May these words serve as a bridge between soul and service, heart and mind, fire and form.

This is my voice, my grief, my joy, and my knowing.
And it is shared now, with you, in Lighted Companionship.

Ω
Table of Contents

Ω

Preface

To Those Who Have Heard the Call,

This work is not the first step upon the Path, nor is it the last.
It is a single transmission in a larger unfolding—a strand of the greater web being woven by Souls around the world who have remembered, who have suffered, and who are now rising.

This book is both a mirror and a map. It reflects my journey—marked by grief, transformation, and direct contact with that inner Flame which neither flickers nor fades. And it offers a map, not to be followed blindly, but to be recognized—as one recognizes a star seen once in a dream, or the voice of a teacher one has not yet met in the flesh.

This text was not written by one who claims mastery. I am not offering you doctrines carved in stone. I am offering you my notes—etched in fire—along the winding ascent into greater service, deeper humility, and bolder love.

Since the writing of my first book, I have passed through a crucible no words could have prepared me for. I lost the one being who saw me in my wholeness—my love, my twin soul, the flame beside mine. That grief did not undo me. It burned me clean. It widened my channel. It refined the Work.

This Codex is the fruit of that fire.

Ω

You will find within these pages the wisdom of the Ageless Teaching, not simply quoted but incarnated. These truths have walked with me, broken me open, and reassembled me in the light of a higher order. I have included my failures. My longings. My awe. I have included the mess of becoming.

For some, this text will be confirmation of what they already know but dared not speak aloud.
For others, it will be the first brush against a deeper current, the beginning of memory returning.

To both, I say: welcome.

I am one among many. A student of the Light, an aspiring servant of Hierarchy, a disciple carrying a lantern lit by lives past and futures approaching. I do not pretend to hold the answers—but I have walked far enough to know how to ask the right questions.

This book is part of an ongoing series—The Entheo Lux Treatises—a chronicle of the inner sciences, the evolving mysteries, and the lived initiations of one striving soul in service to the Plan. It is meant to awaken, to align, to disturb what must be disturbed, and to soothe what has been too long exiled.

If you are reading these words, it is likely that you are ready to take the next step—not alone, but as part of the Group. The New World is being seeded through us. And we are not late.

Ω

Let us walk on, then, together.

In the fire,

W.M.A.

The Lantern Brightens,
The Work Resumes,

And the Way Ahead on the Path becomes Clear.

CHAPTER I

THE SEEKER ON THE PATH

"Learn the meaning of illusion, and in its midst locate the Golden Thread of Truth"

I Call This Holy Place Home

The mountains are, and always have been, my only true refuge from the chaos of the currents—both worldly and astral. For all the strength of the protective shields I've cast around my home, they are still personal creations, woven from the strands of my own will. They cannot compare to the subtle yet immeasurable radiance of Hierarchy that I begin to sense—dimly, reverently—when I am up high. At high altitude it feels easier to become more fully aligned with the Divine Self: the living thread of cosmic tension, the sacred fire from the higher "I Am," streaming through my mental body and anchoring into the center of my heart.

It is within that Heart Chamber—the seat of stillness— where the Master reveals Themselves most clearly. Not through words, but through silence. And within that silence, a voice descends: not to speak over me, but to awaken me. It whispers directly into the spirit, offering access to streams of knowing. Downloads, yes—but only those that correspond to the frequencies I choose through joy, curiosity, and striving. These transmissions are never forced. They arise when I ask for what will further my embodiment of Soul and deepen my ability to serve as a pure stream of insight for others.

The All is becoming real to me now. After years of fragmentation and mystified longing, the surreal is dissolving. The outlines of the Infinite are coming into view—not as visions, but as lived truth. My mind is finally integrating with the Ageless Wisdom. I now carry within me a vocabulary I once lacked, words that can give shape to what I've always known in my Heart but had no language to reveal.

"Always tread carefully," He whispers into my chest.
"And carry Truth to those who seek it."

And I know—they will find me.

Those who are truly seeking what I hold will be magnetized to me by the Law. It is not ambition that drives this Work. It is readiness, recognition, and the field of Right Timing.

This is my Space to fulfill purpose. I have nothing but Time—sacred, infinite, and mine to wield—and no need to rush or place anything above this calling. I can gift myself the stillness of a few open hours, just to let the mind clear, just to receive.

"Meditate the Plan into existence."

W.M.A.

"129 LET US WRITE DOWN QUESTIONS FOR A
DISCIPLE:

'DOST THOU NOT SERVE DARKNESS?
ART THOU NOT A SERVITOR OF DOUBT?
ART THOU NOT A TRAITOR?
ART THOU NOT A LIAR?
ART THOU NOT RIBALD?
ART THOU NOT A SLUGGARD?
ART THOU NOT IRRITABLE?
HAST THOU A TENDENCY TO INCONSTANCY?
ART THOU NOT NEGLIGENT?
DOST THOU UNDERSTAND DEVOTION?
ART THOU READY TO LABOR?
WILT THOU NOT BE AFRAID OF LIGHT?'"

HIERARCHY. THE AGNI YOGA SOCIETY 1931.

From Seeking to Discipleship

To be a seeker is to feel the subtle ache of remembrance before the memory has even returned. It is to sense that something sacred exists just beyond the veil, just behind the noise, and to begin reaching—however clumsily— toward it. This reaching is holy. It marks the first real movement of the Soul within the personality. But seeking alone is not the Path.

Many remain seekers forever. They taste the Light but refuse its demands. They collect fragments of Truth without ever allowing those fragments to shatter the structures they've built around their identity. The seeker is sincere, but still ruled by curiosity. Still hesitant to surrender. Still peering into the Fire, unsure whether to step in.

The aspirant is different. The aspirant has made a vow— spoken or unspoken—to move beyond fascination and into transformation. Their seeking becomes striving. Their curiosity becomes hunger. Their life begins to reorient itself around the flame they once merely admired. The aspirant begins to practice, to purify, to watch the world differently. They feel the gravity of purpose beginning to pull.

But it is the disciple who walks the fire without turning back.

The disciple has ceased to wonder whether they're "on the path." They are the path. Their life becomes the Work. Their personality—while still imperfect—is increasingly obedient to the Soul. They live in rhythm with something greater. They receive instruction. They are tested. They are trusted. And they know that this journey is no longer about personal peace, but planetary service.

It is essential that we each discern where we are in this sequence—not to compare, but to clarify. Because with each stage comes responsibility. The seeker may still play. The aspirant must begin to choose. But the disciple can no longer pretend not to know.

We will now explore these stages more deeply—not as static titles, but as evolutionary states of consciousness. And perhaps, as you read, you will feel something stir—a recognition of where you've been... and a calling toward what you are becoming.

The Seeker, the Aspirant, and the Disciple

The seeker begins by asking questions that the world cannot answer.
"Why am I here?" "What is my purpose?" "What exists beyond death?"
These questions are not signs of confusion, but of awakening. Something stirs behind the mind, whispering of a Reality that cannot be found through pleasure, wealth, or validation. The seeker may dabble in philosophy, in mysticism, in various religions. They may walk through temples, scan through scriptures, attend workshops or pull tarot under the moonlight. But beneath all of this is one thing: a hunger for the Real.

And yet, the seeker still chooses comfort over fire—still turns away when the mirror gets too clear. There is nothing wrong with this. The seeker is in sacred preparation. The soil is being turned. But the time will come when the surface no longer satisfies, and the Soul begins to apply pressure from within.

That pressure creates the aspirant.

The aspirant feels the heat. Something has cracked open. They begin to abandon what is no longer aligned—not just relationships or beliefs, but identities. The aspirant may begin a formal spiritual practice, or return to one with new devotion. They feel a sense of urgency—not frantic, but focused. Time feels different now. They understand that evolution is not optional. That the personality must be purified. That the path is not just about knowing but about becoming.

But the aspirant is still learning how to stand in the fire. Still forgetting and remembering. Still pulled between the higher and the lower. Still tempted to return to the old when the new becomes too demanding. They are not yet a disciple—but they are walking in that direction.

Then something shifts.

The Soul calls—and the aspirant answers. Not with words, but with life. They reorganize their reality. They become disciplined—not in rigidity, but in rhythm. They begin to listen differently. To see symbols in nature. To feel instruction in silence. To observe Hierarchy not as theory, but as Presence.

This is the disciple.

The disciple does not seek power—they carry responsibility. They are not free in the worldly sense, because their life now belongs to the Plan. They serve without applause. They radiate without performance. They strive with joy, and when they fall, they get up faster. The disciple is not perfect—they are in process. But the direction is set. The fire has been accepted. The vow, whether remembered or not, has been made.

Some of you reading this may feel a resonance you cannot explain. A sense that you have moved through these stages before—not just in this life, but across many. That you've sought, aspired, and now... are being asked to commit. If so, let this be a confirmation—not from me, but from the Soul within you. You are ready.

And if you are still seeking—still wandering, still wondering—bless that stage. Bless it with all your heart. Do not rush. Do not force. Just listen, and strive, and ask to be made ready.

Because when the fire comes, it changes everything.

Signs of Transition on the Path

The transition from seeker to aspirant... and from aspirant to disciple... is rarely marked by ceremony. It unfolds silently, gradually, like the turning of a great wheel inside the being. You may not realize it has happened until you look back and see how differently you move, speak, choose, and serve.

But there are signs—quiet confirmations—that a deeper initiation is underway.

⊙ From Seeker to Aspirant:
   • Curiosity becomes longing. You no longer browse truth—you begin to hunger for it.
   • Spiritual dabbling begins to feel empty. You sense the need for depth, structure, and responsibility.
   • Emotional drama loses its charge. You start to recognize your own cycles and respond with greater stillness.
   • The world begins to lose its glamour. Success, pleasure, and validation no longer define your value.
   • You begin simplifying. Not out of rejection, but because excess feels loud against the whisper of Soul.
   • You seek teachers, not personalities. You begin drawing near to Souls who carry fire—not titles.
   • You sense that time is sacred. There is a growing awareness that your incarnation is not casual.

⊙ From Aspirant to Disciple:

- Discipline becomes joy. The practices no longer feel like effort—they feel like home.
- The Will sharpens. You are able to carry through your Soul's intention, even when the personality resists.
- You feel the presence of inner guidance. Dreams, impressions, synchronicities—they begin to instruct you.
- You serve without need for outcome. Your actions are offered upward, without hunger for applause.
- You sense when you're being tested. Life events no longer feel random. You begin seeing the initiatory logic.
- The Work becomes your life. You stop wondering "what your purpose is"—you are living it.
- Hierarchy becomes real. Not a theory, but a Presence. A field you are increasingly aligned with.

These signs are not meant to glorify one stage over another. Each is necessary. Each is sacred. But the transition is real—and when it happens, your life will reflect it. Not in performance, but in precision. Not in titles, but in vibration.

And when the disciple begins to fully live their vow…
they enter the greatest initiation of all:

Service.

To Serve the Plan, Hierarchy, and Shamballa

To serve the Plan is to become more than a person with spiritual interests.
It is to become a living point of contact between heaven and earth.
A bridge. A conduit. A chalice.

It is not glamorous. It is not rewarded in the ways the world teaches.
But it is the most sacred undertaking a Soul can accept.

When we speak of "the Plan," we are not referring to some linear destiny scripted in advance. The Plan is alive. It is the intelligent blueprint of evolution unfolding through humanity, through nature, through light. It exists not as a decree but as a vibration—a pattern of divine thought held within the Mind of the Logos and impressed upon the higher mental plane.

To serve the Plan is to align your life to that current of evolutionary intent. It means surrendering the small self in favor of the greater Work. It means making choices—not from preference, but from resonance. The disciple learns to ask not "what do I want?" but "what will serve?" And then they act with that clarity, even when it costs them comfort.

To serve Hierarchy is to recognize that spiritual authority is real—not in the form of dogma, but in frequency. There are Souls who have gone before us. Masters of Wisdom who have traversed the same path and emerged radiant, exact, selfless, and steady. They do not interfere in petty matters. They do not control. But they watch. They instruct. They bless. They wait for readiness—and they know it when it appears.

Hierarchy is not made up of saviors. It is made up of servants of the Light. They are governed by one law: harmlessness. And they work through one method: radiation. The more you purify, the more you attune to their presence. The more you listen, the more you are guided—not by voice, but by pattern. Hierarchy does not impose. It invites. And to serve it is to become part of that invitation to others.

And then there is Shamballa—the great Center where the Will of God is known.

To serve Shamballa is to serve at the level of Will itself. Not personal willpower, but Divine Will—the pulse of purpose that streams into this system from beyond our comprehension. Shamballa is not a place. It is a plane of planetary intention. To make contact with it is to feel the full voltage of planetary alignment surge through your being. Few are ready for it. But all are called to approach it.

To serve Shamballa is to consecrate your Will to the good of the Whole.
To sacrifice ego-driven ambition.
To wield fire without attachment.
To become unshakable—not in hardness, but in clarity.

The disciple who serves the Plan becomes magnetic.
The disciple who serves Hierarchy becomes luminous.

The disciple who serves Shamballa becomes a flame in motion.

And these are not separate. They are stages of deepening.
The Plan is the outer structure.
Hierarchy is the guiding presence.
Shamballa is the Source.

The true disciple does not merely study the Plan. They embody it.
They do not worship Hierarchy. They align with it.
They do not chase Shamballa. They surrender to its call and build the body that can bear its flame.

This is what it means to serve—not as martyr, not as fanatic, not as superior—but as one who has remembered their purpose and now chooses to live as a sacred instrument of Light.

To the Student on the Way

To you, dear traveler—whether you are just now taking your first conscious step or have walked lifetimes through flame—I honor your arrival.

This book found you for a reason. Not because you are lost, but because you are ready. Ready to remember what you already carry. Ready to align more fully with the thread of Light that has always been whispering through your being. You don't need to rush. You don't need to be perfect. But you are invited—deeply, lovingly—to become available.

Available to the Soul.
Available to Hierarchy.
Available to the Plan.

Whatever doubts you carry, let them be placed on the altar of aspiration. Whatever shadows still swirl, let them be viewed with honesty but without shame. You are becoming. You are unfolding. And that unfolding is sacred.

The path of the disciple is not a performance. It is a purification. And in that process, there will be grief, yes—but also grace. You are not alone. The presence of the Masters surrounds you. The light of your Solar Angel awaits your attention. The fire within you is not theoretical. It is real. And with each breath, each step, each act of alignment—you stoke it.

This Codex is not just something to read. It is something to enter. Let it speak not only to your intellect, but to your intuition. Let it bypass your expectations and touch the place within you that has always known...
that this life is holy,
that your time is now,
and that you came here to serve.

W.M.A.

An Invocation of the Light of the Soul

I stand in the Light of the Soul.
I call upon the Flame within.
I surrender what is false.
I awaken what is true.

May the fire purify me.
May the Will strengthen me.
May the Plan reveal itself through me.

I offer myself as a servant of the Light.
I remember my place within the Great Chain.
I walk forward—not alone, but aligned.

May the Forces of Light illuminate the way.
May the Masters guide my steps.
May the Will of Shamballa be done—
through me,
in me,
and all around me.

So let it be.

Further Reflection

The goal is not mere comfort or personal success, but the manifestation of the Kingdom of the Soul upon Earth—a realm where Freedom, Light, Love, Liberty, and Peace flow in ordered abundance. These are not abstract ideals. They are emanations of the Plan. And the principle that binds them—draws them into coherence and manifestation—is what the Ageless Wisdom names Pure Reason: the radiance of Mind united with Love, guided by Will, and aligned with the Whole.

Call forth now the invisible treasury of your lineage—the wealth not measured in coin, but in accumulated light. The royal blood of your forebears flows through the veins of your Spirit, crowned not by conquest but by conscious striving. If you have felt the summons, if you have remembered your vow, then yes—you are royalty. Not of empire, but of emanation. Call your true empire into form. Not through domination, but through radiant alignment.

I repeat this invocation as a sacred utterance—
A mantric declaration that fuels my Work:
"May my Empire of Education, Science, and Spirituality manifest."
Not for myself, but as a vessel through which the Light of Hierarchy may shape new culture.

In my previous writings, I recounted a dream—a vision—and a vow made to the Inner Government of the World. Despite all outer circumstance, I know this vow is binding. A thread was spun in that moment, and I will be held to it. The mission entrusted to this Temple is not symbolic. It is real. It is to restore the memory of spiritual technology to the Earth. The ancient ruins that dot our world, long reduced to myth or superstition, are not silent. They pulse with untapped functions—energetic harmonics, nodal intelligences, and sacred geometries interwoven with the Earth's own etheric body. The ley lines are not legend. They are the nervous system of Gaia.

But humanity has forgotten. The memory of the Planetary Life—the vast Being in whose body we live—has dimmed, replaced by fractured doctrine and fearful worship. The great heresy of separation has been institutionalized, teaching us that Divinity is elsewhere, external, guarded by clergy or confined to scripture. This is the true blasphemy—to believe that one must be granted permission to return to Source.

These patterns of worship belong to the waning age.
We now enter Aquarius—the Sign of the World Server—and must bear its responsibility. The influence of Capricorn, streaming just behind it, calls us to lead, to educate, and to govern with Light. Aquarius pours the water of consciousness from the vessel of the Soul, while Capricorn constructs the initiatory structures through which that water may flow with precision.

This is not mythology. This is the esoteric architecture of evolution. The bridge to the Golden World is already under construction.

Look around. See clearly. The destruction playing out across systems and structures is not senseless—it is sacred combustion. A karmic releasing. The tension that has been mounting since the early 20th century now finds release as the Old Order collapses under the pressure of the incoming Light. This is not the end of civilization. It is the initiation of a planetary society. And as with all initiations, the former self must burn to clear space for the Real.

The ashes of fallen temples are not waste. They are the foundation stones of new sanctuaries. The future will not rise on fantasy, but on the refined remnants of what we've outgrown. Wisdom reclaims its form.

And so I offer these words not as prediction, but as a call to inner attunement. Read them not only with intellect, but with the eye of the Heart. These truths are layered. Their purpose is not to instruct the surface mind, but to open the gate of recognition within the Soul.

All is not as it seems.
All is exactly as it must be.

W.M.A.

The Path of the Initiate

At a certain point upon the Path, the distinctions between seeker, aspirant, and disciple begin to blur—not because the stages cease to exist, but because the inner life merges more completely with the higher will. There arises a new quality, subtle at first, then steadily deepening: the quality of the Initiate.

An Initiate is not simply a disciple who has achieved a technical milestone or who has "graduated" from worldly concerns. The process of initiation, as taught throughout the Ageless Wisdom, is not the conferring of spiritual honor—it is the conscious assumption of spiritual responsibility. It marks a definite, scientific expansion of consciousness, a step-by-step awakening of the latent faculties of the Soul and Spirit within form.

In the Treatise on Cosmic Fire, we are told that initiation is "an expansion of the consciousness—an expansion which is the result of the definite, voluntary effort, and the struggle of the inner man to control, purify, and refine his lower bodies." It is the natural, inevitable unfolding of the divine seed within each one of us, when ripened by service, self-mastery, and a burning aspiration to align with the Plan.

Initiates are those who have passed beyond the glamorous mist of personality identification. Their orientation is no longer toward fulfillment of the little self, but toward fulfillment of divine purpose. Yet, paradoxically, the true Initiate remains the simplest of beings: a server, a brother or sister to all, a vessel for greater light.

It must be remembered that initiation is both an interior and a hierarchical process. Internally, it is a revelation of one's own divine potential—a lifting of the veil between the lower and higher self. Externally, it is the recognition by Hierarchy that the aspirant has earned the right to consciously wield greater energies in service to the Plan. The Masters do not impose initiation; they merely open the door when the disciple has built it through living service and sacrificial love.

The paths of the seeker, the aspirant, and the disciple are the preparation ground. They are stages of growing alignment, of progressive integration, of greater magnetic pull toward the Soul and its Source. All of these stages overlap and spiral back upon one another, for the path is not linear—it is a living, breathing expansion.

At any moment, one may be simultaneously a seeker in one aspect of life, an aspirant in another, and a disciple in a third. The path is a continuum of unfoldment, marked not by outer achievement, but by inner luminosity: the increasing radiance of the Soul's fire through the lower bodies.

When the Soul's light begins to dominate the field of consciousness, the First Initiation looms near. The will to tread the Path firmly, no matter the cost, is sealed within the heart. It is here that the title of Initiate is first truly earned—not by proclamation, but by the silent testimony of a life becoming flame.

And yet, the Initiate remains a disciple, ever learning, ever purifying, ever surrendering selfhood into greater wholes. As Light on the Path reminds us: "Kill out ambition. Kill out desire of life. Yet work as those who love life. Respect life as those who desire it."

The journey does not end with Initiation; it intensifies. Each true initiation brings a fuller contact with the higher Triad—the pure Light of Spirit—and a greater obligation to carry that Light into the darkest corners of the world.

Thus, we are all upon the same spiral path—some running ahead, some stumbling behind, but all moving inevitably toward the flame from which we were born.

It is to this sacred process of Initiation that we now turn.

The Five Human Initiations: Gates of Consciousness

There comes a moment, somewhere along the twisting path of seeking, when the soul realizes it is not simply wandering through life — it is ascending through ordered gates, ancient and invisible, that have been known to the Wise Ones of every age. These are the Five Initiations of the Ageless Wisdom: markers of profound transformation, of death and rebirth, not of the body but of consciousness itself.

Initiation is not a reward. It is not given as a trophy for devotion or study. It is a natural flowering, a blossoming of the inner fire that has long been tended in secret through lifetimes of striving, failing, and rising again. As A Treatise on Cosmic Fire reminds us:

"Initiation is the beginning of a process which must be voluntarily and consciously undertaken until it culminates in full union with the Will aspect of Divinity."

These five initiations chart the soul's gradual transfiguration—step by step—from prisoner of matter to conscious Son of the Flame.

The First Initiation: Birth into the Kingdom of Souls

In the ancient texts, this moment is called the Birth of the Christ within the heart—not a religious event, but a spiritual reality. It is here that the light of the Soul first pierces the darkness of the lower nature with permanence.

The seeker, having fought for basic mastery over the physical body and its demands, begins to radiate a steady light. No longer is life driven by instinct alone. A quiet dignity arises—an impulse toward service, purity, and harmlessness.

The body becomes an instrument of the Soul's will. In The Secret Doctrine, Blavatsky speaks of this awakening as the "first quickening of the inner Self," the moment when the divine life stirs unmistakably in the mortal shell.

This first gate marks not an ending, but a beginning: the conscious assumption of spiritual responsibility.

The Second Initiation: Baptism by the Waters

As progress continues, the aspirant faces the surging tides of the emotional world. At the second initiation, often termed the "Baptism," it is not the body that must be mastered, but the waters of emotion—the stormy seas of desire, fear, anger, and attachment.

Here, the aspirant must stand steady amidst the flood, neither driven by passion nor drowned by despair. The waters must become calm, reflective, and receptive to the higher Light.

Cosmic Fire correlates this stage with the awakening influence of the fire of mind—reason and intuition beginning to still the chaos of the astral plane. Desire is transmuted into aspiration; personal wants are slowly replaced by the magnetic pull of the greater Good.

The second initiation is hard-won. It demands inner honesty and a deepening of self-discipline—but it also brings the first true taste of spiritual freedom.

The Third Initiation: The Transfiguration

If the first two initiations are about mastery of form, the third is about the revelation of identity.

Here, the entire lower nature—physical, emotional, and mental—is brought into unified service under the Soul's direction. The disciple stands revealed as a soul-infused being, radiant and clear, no longer ruled by the separative self.

This is the "Transfiguration" of biblical allegory. It is the stage at which the causal body—the soul's vehicle on the higher mental plane—begins to disintegrate, for its work of bridging Spirit and matter is largely done.

The Secret Doctrine hints at this stage, speaking of the "Self-becoming Self," when the spiritual Triad—the higher mind, intuition, and spiritual will—begins to overshadow the soul itself.

Those who pass this gate become true World Servers, radiating not personality charisma but the magnetic power of the soul's Purpose.

The Fourth Initiation: The Great Renunciation

The fourth initiation is often called the most difficult of all. It is the crucifixion—not of flesh, but of attachment. Even attachment to the Soul itself must be relinquished.

The initiate stands alone upon the mountain, stripped of all lesser identities, all cherished forms, all desires for reward, recognition, or even spiritual progress. What remains is Will—the pure, inexorable Will of the Spirit, flowing through an empty and consecrated vessel.

At this stage, A Treatise on Cosmic Fire states:

"The will of the initiate merges with the Will of the Planetary Logos. He becomes, consciously, a part of the greater Purpose."

Few reach this gate in any single lifetime, but for those who do, a profound liberation follows. They become conscious agents of Shamballa, no longer seeking salvation for themselves, but operating entirely for the salvation of worlds.

The Fifth Initiation: Resurrection into the Greater Life

Beyond the Crucifixion lies the Resurrection.

The fifth initiation marks full entry into the spiritual Kingdom—the true Home of the liberated soul. The initiate becomes a Master of Wisdom, a co-creator with the divine Plan, no longer bound to the wheel of human reincarnation unless choosing to serve.

Cosmic Fire describes this stage as the complete identification of the lower triad (mind, emotions, body) with the higher Triad (atma, buddhi, manas). The soul is no longer an intermediary—it has been transcended. Spirit acts directly through matter.

The Master does not escape life, but returns again and again, radiating light into the darkest places, carrying the seed of future civilizations.

A Path Beyond the Known

It is important to remember that the five initiations are not an ending. They are a beginning—the threshold of a far vaster journey across cosmic streams and solar destinies.

As The Secret Doctrine so beautifully hints:

"The spark of Divine Flame becomes the beacon guiding worlds yet unborn."

Every seeker reading these words—every struggling soul striving toward greater light—is already moving toward these gates. The rhythm of life itself carries us forward: from the instinct of the animal, to the intuition of the human, to the inspiration of the divine.

The path is steep. It demands sacrifice, courage, and relentless self-forgetfulness. But it also promises a reward beyond comprehension: to become a conscious flame within the greater Fire, a living bridge between worlds, a joyful participant in the unfolding Plan of the Logos.

In the end, there is no external judge barring the way. The true gates are opened only by the fire you cultivate within your own heart.

The Five Human Initiations; A Summary

First Initiation – Birth:

The Soul's light awakens permanently within the heart.
The physical body is disciplined and brought under
conscious control, becoming an instrument of spiritual
purpose.

Second Initiation – Baptism:

The turbulent waters of the emotional body are purified
and stilled. Desire gives way to aspiration, and the astral
body becomes a clear reflector of the Soul's intention.

Third Initiation – Transfiguration:

The personality—body, emotions, and lower mind—is
unified and wholly infused by the Soul. The true spiritual
identity emerges, radiant and selfless, in service to
humanity.

Fourth Initiation – Renunciation:

All attachments, even to Soul identity, are surrendered.
The initiate merges consciously with divine Will,
becoming a pure channel for the Purpose held in the
Heart of Shamballa.

Fifth Initiation – Resurrection:

The Soul itself is transcended. The Master of Wisdom arises, liberated from personal karma, standing as a conscious co-creator within the planetary evolution.

"The Way leads from darkness to Light, from the unreal to the Real, and from death to Immortality."

-

-Ageless Wisdom Teaching

W.M.A.

-

CHAPTER II

MEDITATION AND THE LIGHT OF THE SOUL

"Meditation is the ladder to the Triad; through it, the Dweller is faced, and the Angel revealed."

The Bridge of Flame

There comes a time, often quietly and without announcement, when yearning alone no longer suffices. The mystic, radiant in devotion and softened by longing, feels a subtle prompting—an inner instruction whispered from the soul itself—to take the next step. This chapter marks that threshold.

We stand now at the juncture where love must become knowledge, where the ineffable must be examined through a new faculty of mind, refined not by thought alone but by fire—by intuition lit through discipline. No longer content with momentary glimpses or emotional ascent, the seeker becomes the student of Reality itself, bending their whole being to the rigors of union through realization. The longing that once carried them into fleeting encounters with the Divine must now be shaped into a focused, steady alignment.

This is the path of occult meditation—not the passive retreat of the mystic, but the active labor of the soul as it reaches inward and upward toward synthesis. It is not an abandonment of the heart's devotion, but the fulfillment of that devotion through the lighted mind. The beloved becomes not merely yearned for, but known. The door does not swing open by longing alone—it opens through preparation, purification, and precise application of the mind's higher function: revelation.

We begin here to explore the transition from the illumined mystic to the occult disciple, from adoration to union, from perception to conscious integration. The laws of the higher worlds beckon. The soul awaits recognition. The path ahead is steep—but glorious. And you, dear reader, are ready.

Let us now listen to the wisdom of From Intellect to Intuition, and reflect deeply on the transformation that leads from mysticism into mastery.

W.M.A.

Excerpt:
From Intellect to Intuition
A.A.B.

But the mystical way is a preparation for the way of knowledge and where the mystic stops in adoration of the vision and in yearning after the Beloved, the seeker after true knowledge takes up the task and carries the work forward...

This thought confines the whole idea within the realm of sensuous perception, but there is something more. There is direct knowledge. There is an understanding of the laws governing this new realm of being. There is submission to a new procedure and to those steps and passwords which lead to the door and procure its opening. It is here that meditation plays its part and the mind steps in to fulfill its new function of revelation. Through meditation, the union for which the mystic yearns, and which he senses, and of which he has brief and fleeting experience, becomes definite and is known past all controversy, being recoverable at will...

To take the Mind and bend it to its new task as a revealer of the divine is now the objective of the convinced mystic. To do this with success and with happiness, he will need a clear vision of his goal and a lucid understanding of the results eventually to be demonstrated. He will need a keen formulation of the assets with which he approaches his endeavor, and an equally keen appreciation of his lacks and defects. A view, as balanced as may be, of himself and of his circumstances, should be gained. Paralleling this, however, there should be also an equally balanced view of the goal and an understanding of the wonder of the realizations and gifts which will be his, when his interest has been transferred from the things that now engross his attention, and his emotions, to the more esoteric values and standards.

We have touched upon the point that meditation is a process whereby the mind is reoriented to Reality, and, rightly used, can lead a man into another kingdom in nature, into another state of consciousness and Being and into another dimension. The goal of achievement has shifted into higher realms of thought and realization.

What are the definite results of this reorientation?

It might be stated first of all that meditation is the science which enables us to arrive at direct experience of God. That in which we live and move and have our being is no longer the object of aspiration, or a symbol to us of a divine possibility. We know God as the Eternal Cause and the source of all that is, including ourselves.

We recognize the Whole. We become one with God by becoming one with our own immortal soul, and when that tremendous event takes place we find that the consciousness of the individual soul is the consciousness of the whole, and that separateness and division, distinctions and the concepts of me and thee, of God and a child of God, have faded away in the knowledge and realization of unity.

Dualism has given place to unity.

This is the Way of Union. The integrated Personality has been transcended through an ordered process of soul unfoldment, and a conscious at-one-ment has been brought about between the lower or personal self and the higher or divine self."

From Intellect to Intuition
A.A.B.

The Sacred Science

To speak truly of meditation is to speak of a sacred science. It is not merely a practice or a calming ritual, though it may begin as such. It is, in its most profound essence, the key by which the seeker may unlock the inner temple and enter into conscious communion with the Soul. And beyond the Soul, meditation becomes the bridge to the Monad itself—the pure spiritual spark that is the origin and ultimate destination of each individualized consciousness.

Most aspirants begin upon the path of meditation through the influence of the personality life. There is desire for peace, healing, clarity, or perhaps communion with the divine as it is understood emotionally or devotionally. This marks the way of the mystic, and is a noble and necessary phase. However, the mystic must eventually become the occultist, and the longing of the heart must fuse with the directed light of the mind. When this fusion is achieved, the personality no longer leads, but is led. The light of the Soul begins to permeate the emotional and mental fields, casting out illusion, glamour, and maya with the fire of clarity.

To meditate rightly is to orient the entire lower nature towards that inner sun of the Soul, and to allow its radiance to purify, align, and ultimately transform the vehicle of expression into a conduit for divine purpose. This is no small task, and it does not occur quickly. It is the work of lives. And yet, in this life, you may make measurable progress if you will it and if you persist with faith and discipline.

As the light of the Soul begins to stream down, illuminating the mind and bringing order to the emotional nature, a shift begins to occur. The lower self becomes increasingly aware of the presence of the higher self, and this presence grows until it becomes a living reality within the consciousness. It is here that the true work of occult meditation begins. One no longer meditates to receive blessings or visions, but to participate consciously in the Plan.

The Solar Angel, that radiant intermediary who has overseen the evolution of the Soul since its descent into form, now becomes a conscious guide and companion. This Angel is not the Soul itself, but the bridge-builder— the architect of the causal body and the lighted path upward. Through the work of meditation, the light of the Solar Angel begins to reflect more clearly through the aura of the disciple, stimulating not only insight, but action. The Soul is not passive. It seeks expression. And through meditation, the Soul's will becomes known.

However, between the personality and the Soul lies the Dweller on the Threshold. This Dweller is the composite of all that has not yet been redeemed: fear, pride, desire for separateness, the residue of past errors and the inertia of ancient habits. As the light of the Soul grows stronger, it casts a sharper contrast upon this Dweller, and the disciple is forced to confront all that stands between them and full Soul alignment. This confrontation is part of the initiation process, and no true occult meditation path is complete without it.

Many turn back at this point, mistaking the rising of the Dweller as failure. But it is a sign of progress, for one must know the enemy within in order to conquer it. The light reveals what must be transmuted. The fire of the Soul does not destroy the Dweller—it transforms it. Meditation becomes the forge in which the personality is refined, tested, and ultimately reoriented towards divine service.

Beyond the Soul lies the Monad—that mysterious, brilliant point of spiritual origin which the Soul itself reflects. Few reach this high point of contact in a single lifetime, yet all meditation paths, when rightly pursued, ultimately lead there. The Monad is the source of the divine will within you. It is the Father in Heaven, the pure flame of Spirit. Through advanced meditation and initiation, the disciple eventually comes into conscious rapport with this essence. When the Monad is touched, all prior perceptions of unity and purpose are magnified beyond comprehension.

This is why occult meditation is more than a technique. It is a system of scientific spiritual unfoldment. It is the science of aligning the personality with the Soul, the Soul with the Monad, and ultimately the Monad with the One Life. It involves purification, intention, intelligent application of mental power, and the cultivation of detachment, serenity, and sacrificial will.

Each true meditation becomes an act of service, a sounding of the Soul's note into the world. Over time, the disciple becomes less concerned with personal illumination and more attuned to what the Soul seeks to express through them in service to the Plan.

To the reader, I say this: begin where you are. If you meditate in longing, good. If you meditate in silence, better. If you meditate with intention to align and serve, you are already upon the way.

The time is now to shift from seeking the Light to *becoming* the Light. The Light of the Soul is not a metaphor. It is a literal, measurable force that becomes increasingly tangible as the work proceeds. That Light is your birthright, and its purpose is not for private attainment, but for planetary transformation.

Let your meditation carry you ever inward and upward. Let it carry you into the fire that purifies, into the light that reveals, and into the silence where the voice of the Soul may finally be heard.

Let it carry you home.

W.M.A.

Meditation as Occult Process: The Science of Soul Contact

Meditation is not merely a tool for personal peace or a practice of mystical devotion; it is a method of occult alignment—a precise science, born of the Ageless Wisdom, by which the seeker may ascend the ladder of consciousness and become a living channel for the Divine Plan.

In *Letters on Occult Meditation*, Alice Bailey makes clear that meditation is the "ordered process of becoming aware of the Real, the Beautiful, and the True." It is a graded practice of transforming mental substance, of organizing the etheric and astral bodies, and of clearing the channel between the mind and the Soul so that energy may flow without obstruction. Meditation, when practiced correctly, is a laboratory of consciousness, and the disciple its devoted scientist.

This sacred science functions on several levels: as purification, as invocation, as radiation, and ultimately, as union. The mystic yearns for union and may experience moments of bliss, but the occultist knows the steps that build the permanent bridge—the antahkarana—between the lower and higher self. This is the great work of occult meditation: the construction of the rainbow bridge that unites the personal with the spiritual, the temporal with the eternal.

The Role of the Mind and the Building of the Antahkarana

The mind is both a veil and a vehicle. At first, it veils the Soul's radiance with its endless fluctuations. Later, it becomes the vehicle through which the Soul expresses itself. When used rightly, the mind becomes the directing agent of the Soul's purpose, able to focus light with precision.

Bailey states, "The building of the antahkarana is the result of the meditative life." Each correct meditation deposits energy within the upper mind, strengthening the connection between manas (lower mind) and buddhi (Soul intuition). This bridge is not imaginary—it is energetic and real, woven of currents and impressions consciously received and anchored. Over lifetimes, this bridge becomes the path by which the Monad, the originating spark of divinity, impresses its Will upon the incarnate disciple.

The Monad: The Flame Beyond the Soul

In the secret teachings, the Monad is the divine seed, the eternal spark from which all individuality emerges. It is the source of pure Will and Love-Wisdom—our truest identity beyond form, emotion, and even thought. As Blavatsky writes in *The Secret Doctrine*, the Monad is "the indivisible point of spirit," and it is from this point that the journey of return is initiated.

Occult meditation, when pursued beyond the stage of Soul contact, aims to bring the disciple into rapport with this Monad. This process does not occur through emotional yearning or visualization alone, but through silent, sustained contact achieved by aligning the mental body with buddhi and ultimately with atma, the spiritual will. The Arcane School teaches that when one touches the Monad, one becomes a radiatory point of spiritual Will in the world—a true white magician.

The Dweller on the Threshold and the Test of Fire

Before the Soul can pour its full light through the personality, the Dweller on the Threshold must be confronted. This composite shadow, built from unredeemed thought-forms, karmic residue, and subconscious fears, stands guard before the gate of higher initiation. Meditation accelerates the surfacing of this Dweller, not to punish, but to offer the opportunity for transmutation.

This process may feel like psychological crisis. It may manifest as emotional upheaval, deep questioning, or the confrontation of long-buried shadows. This is why meditation must be approached with reverence and training—it is a fire that burns, not a balm that soothes. Yet this fire is redemptive. It is through this very confrontation that the personality is purified and brought into alignment with the Soul's rhythm.

Bailey writes, "The Dweller on the Threshold must be seen, known and recognised for what it is before the Angel of the Presence can shine forth in all its glory." The Dweller is not evil—it is simply everything we have left undone. And meditation is the instrument that reveals what must be done.

The Solar Angel and the Descent of Light

The Solar Angel is the divine intermediary. It is the guide, the architect of the causal body, the bringer of light from the higher worlds. The Angel is not a mythic being, but a real and living intelligence, sacrificed from the higher deva evolution to oversee human soul evolution. As Blavatsky hints, and Bailey confirms, this radiant being has "waited patiently" through centuries of incarnation, preparing the disciple for the moment of conscious communion.

When occult meditation is stabilized, and the Dweller is faced and gradually integrated, the Solar Angel begins to impress its purpose with greater clarity. Visions become replaced by directives. Intuition overtakes inspiration. The disciple becomes a server, not for their own sake, but as an agent of the Plan.

The descent of light is literal. The aura changes. The chakras realign. The very presence of the meditator becomes magnetic and healing. The Plan begins to use the vehicle.

The Effects of Meditation: Objective and Measurable

As this process unfolds, certain effects become observable, both within and without:

- A deepening serenity, regardless of outer events.

- A clarified sense of purpose and direction.

- Increased sensitivity to the suffering and needs of others.

- Sharpened mental faculties and creative inspiration.

- A tendency toward service, simplicity, and synthesis.

Eventually, the higher initiations are approached. Through meditation, the causal body—the storehouse of Soul memory—is gradually dismantled, and the light of the Monad begins to pour through. The disciple enters into the greater mystery: not only of becoming a Soul, but of becoming a living flame of divine Will.

A Closing Thought for the Disciple

You are not simply meant to meditate. You are meant to become meditation.

The Soul is calling not for ritual, but for radiation. Each moment of true alignment becomes a beacon. The science is precise, and the path is charted. Thousands have walked it before you. You are not alone.

As you turn inward with disciplined thought and upward with sacred intent, the doors begin to open. One by one, the veils part. And behind each, a greater light.

Let meditation not be the act of seeking light, but the act of being light. Let the Angel come. Let the Dweller rise. Let the Monad be known.

And let the fire descend.

W.M.A.

The Living Fire of Silence

When all techniques are exhausted and the effort itself dissolves into serenity, what remains is the sacred stillness of the Soul in full communion with its Source. This stillness is not emptiness—it is radiant presence. It is the quiet pulse of Spirit that underlies all manifestation and sings in the silence between thoughts.

The disciple, seasoned through the fires of aspiration and purified by the waters of devotion, eventually arrives at the threshold where meditation becomes not a doing, but a state of being. Here, meditation is no longer something one performs; it is something one becomes. The meditating mind has merged with the Soul's intention. The heart has been cleansed of illusion. The body has been made a living temple. This is the goal of all true esoteric practice: to become an instrument of divine Will in the world.

Alice Bailey wrote, "Meditation is the method of the trained occultist; prayer is the method of the mystic." In the fusion of these two lies the evolution of humanity's next great spiritual leap. The mystic yearns, the occultist directs; together they form the triangle through which the fire of the higher worlds may descend.

True occult meditation lifts the seeker beyond the realms of desire and identification with form. It refines the mental body into a mirror, capable of reflecting the archetypes of divine thought into practical, transformative action. The personality is no longer the protagonist of one's journey, but the steward. The Soul no longer whispers from behind a veil—it radiates from within, evident in one's presence, speech, and service.

This chapter would not be complete without recognition of the role of the Great Ones who stand behind the evolution of consciousness on this planet. Every act of meditation performed with pure intent becomes a call to the Hierarchy, a sounding forth of one's readiness to serve. And each such call is met with response, though not always in ways expected. The Master does not always speak in visions or dreams; sometimes the guidance arrives as clarity, as a new strength of will, or as the sudden dissolving of a once-insurmountable obstacle.

The bridge from the personality to the Soul, and from the Soul to the Monad, is built of living light. Each time the disciple enters silence with sincerity, more light is woven into that bridge. One day, that bridge will be fully constructed, and the lower self will stand no more as a shadow, but as a luminous extension of Spirit. That is the goal. That is the path.

To the reader who walks this way: the journey is sacred, and your striving matters. Each morning you face the world with intention to serve is a note added to the symphony of the Soul. Each time you choose silence over reaction, truth over illusion, alignment over ego—something within you becomes more permanent, more radiant, more real.

Take heart. The Masters have walked this way before us. The Soul has not forgotten you. The Monad calls from within the silence. And meditation is the sacred key that unlocks the door.

May your meditations reveal your highest purpose, ignite your deepest devotion, and link you ever more surely to the Living Light that streams forth from the center where the Will of God is known.

So let it be.

W.M.A.

CHAPTER III

THE HIDDEN GOVERNMENT OF EARTH:

AN INTRODUCTION TO THE PLANETARY HIERARCHY

*"Behind all world events, the Silent Watchers stand—
guiding evolution with a Will beyond our knowing.
From Shamballa flows the Will of God; through
Hierarchy, it is translated into Light for the world."*

A Formal Introduction to the Planetary Hierarchy

Before we enter into the excerpted teachings from *Initiation, Human and Solar* by Alice A. Bailey, let us take a moment to prepare the ground of understanding. We are not simply discussing organizational structures of a spiritual order—we are being invited into the **living architecture of divine governance** on this planet. The Hierarchy is not an abstraction. It is not a theory. It is a **living organism**, composed of fully awakened Souls who have transcended the human condition and now function as **conscious co-workers with the Plan of Evolution.**

This Hierarchy—sometimes called the Great White Brotherhood, the Inner Government, or simply the Elder Brothers—is composed of Initiates and Masters who have achieved a level of development that allows them to guide the evolution of humanity from the inner planes. Their presence is not imposed. It is offered, radiated, and aligned with the Law of Free Will. Yet their impact is profound.

The Hierarchy is organized into **three major departments**, each representing one aspect of the Divine Trinity, and each governed by a great Lord or Chohan:

The Department of the Manu

First Ray – Will and Power

The Manu is the expression of the Will of God as it pertains to humanity's racial, social, and cultural evolution. This department governs the **structural formation of civilization**—its root races, its nations, its physical forms and tendencies. The Manu does not work through emotional persuasion or mental reasoning but through the **ordering force of divine will**. It is through the Manu's guidance that the **archetypes of future humanity** are selected and seeded into form. On a global level, the Department of the Manu oversees the rise and fall of civilizations in accordance with karmic law and planetary necessity.

In terms of initiation, this ray conditions the **Path of the Occultist**—those who walk the Way of Power, of order, of exactitude, and silent impact. The Manu works closely with the Lords of Karma, the planetary Builders, and those disciples whose service lies in political, structural, or geographic influence.

The Department of the World Teacher

Second Ray – Love-Wisdom
The Lord Maitreya, known in various traditions as the Christ, the Bodhisattva, the Imam Mahdi, or the Kalki Avatar, currently holds the office of World Teacher. This department is the **heart center of the Hierarchy**, and its primary function is to **infuse humanity with the consciousness of Love**—not sentimentality, but the **unifying force of Divine Wisdom.**

The World Teacher guides the work of the great world religions, the awakening of group consciousness, and the gradual **externalization of the Christ Consciousness** into the mental and emotional bodies of humanity. This department presides over those whose path lies through **devotion, synthesis, healing, teaching, and creative unity.**

In terms of initiation, this ray conditions the **Path of the Mystic and the Healer.** Many in the New Group of World Servers respond primarily to this current. As the Aquarian energies intensify, the Second Ray will become increasingly dominant, leading to a **reconciliation between science and spirituality**, mind and heart.

The Department of the Mahachohan

Third Ray – Active Intelligence (and Rays 4 through 7)
The Mahachohan is sometimes called the Lord of Civilization or the Lord of Culture. This office synthesizes the **creative rays** (3, 4, 5, 6, and 7) and distributes them through the **subtle bodies of the Earth**. It is the Mahachohan's department that governs the arts, science, philosophy, language, and the intricate patterns of human interaction.

Through this office flow the energies that manifest as **scientific innovation, ritual magic, cultural renaissance, and intellectual progress**. It is also through this department that ceremonial magic, esoteric schools, and occult ritual are administered. It is the most complex department, containing within it multiple Ray ashrams and coordinating a wide range of planetary functions.

Those aligned with this ray structure often walk the **Path of the Magician, the Philosopher, the Artist, or the Scientist**, depending on their soul's ray configuration. It is the department that governs the **seventh ray ceremonial order** that is rising in this present age.

The interplay of these three rays—Will, Love-Wisdom, and Active Intelligence—forms the **triadic flame of planetary evolution**. Every Soul on the Path, knowingly or not, resonates primarily with one of these great departments. As you read the following excerpt, consider this: which of these rays calls to you? Which current resonates most in your service? You need not choose—but in recognizing the

Ψ

pull, you may begin to better understand your own rhythm within the Whole.

Now, with reverence, let us proceed into the sacred architecture of the Hierarchy, as offered by the Tibetan through Alice A. Bailey.

W.M.A.

Excerpt
Initiation, Human and Solar
A.A.B.

The Three Departments of Hierarchy

Standing around the Lord of the World, but withdrawn and esoteric, are three more Kumaras, Who make the seven of planetary manifestation. Their work is to us necessarily obscure. The three exoteric Buddhas, or Kumaras, are the sum-total of activity or planetary energy, and the three esoteric Kumaras embody types of energy which as yet are not in full demonstration upon our planet.

Each of these six Kumaras is a reflection of, and the distributing agent for, the energy and force of one of the six other Planetary Logoi, the remaining six spirits before the Throne. Sanat Kumara alone, in this scheme, is self-sustaining and self-sufficient, being the physical incarnation of one of the Planetary Logoi, which one it is not permissible to state, as this fact is one of the secrets of initiation. Through each of Them passes the life force of one of the six rays, and in considering Them one might sum up Their work and position as follows:—

1. They each embody one of the six types of energy, with the Lord of the World as the synthesizer and the embodier of the perfect seventh type, our planetary type.

2. They are each distinguished by one of the six color, with the Lord of the World showing forth the full planetary color, these six being subsidiary.

3. Their work is therefore concerned, not only with force distribution, but with the passing into our scheme from other planetary schemes, of Egos seeking earth experience.

4. Each of Them is in direct communication with one or another of the sacred planets.

5. According to astrological conditions, and according to the turning of the planetary wheel of life, so one or another of these Kumaras will be active. The three Buddhas of Activity change from time to time, and become in turn exoteric or esoteric as the case may be.

Only the King persists steadily and watchfully in active physical incarnation.

Besides these main presiding Personalities in the Council Chamber at Shamballa, there is a group of four Beings Who are the representatives upon the planet of the four Maharajas, or the four Lords of Karma in the solar system, who are specifically concerned with the evolution at the present time of the human kingdom. These four are connected with:—

1. The distribution of karma, or human destiny, as it affects individuals, and through the individuals, the groups.

2. The care and tabulation of the akashic records. They are concerned with the Halls of Records, or with the "keeping of the book," as it is called in the Christian Bible;

They are known in the Christian world as the recording angels.

3. The participation in solar councils. They alone have the right during the world cycle to pass beyond the periphery of the planetary scheme, and participate in the councils of the Solar Logos. Thus They are literally planetary mediators, representing our Planetary Logos and all that concerns Him in the greater scheme of which He is but a part.

Co-operating with these karmic Lords are the large groups of initiates and devas who occupy themselves with the right adjustment of:—

a. World karma,
b. Racial karma,
c. National karma,
d. Group karma,
e. Individual karma,

and who are responsible to the Planetary Logos for the correct manipulation of those forces and building agencies which bring in the right Egos on the different rays at the correct times and seasons.

With all these groups we have little concern, for they are contacted only by initiates of the third initiation, and by those of even more exalted rank.

The Work of the Manu.

The Manu presides over group one. He is called Vaivasvata Manu, and is the Manu of the fifth root-race. He is the ideal man or thinker, and sets the type for our Aryan race, having presided over its destinies since its inception nearly one hundred thousand years ago. Other Manus have come and gone and His place will be, in the relatively near future, taken by someone else. He will then pass on to other work of a more exalted kind. The Manu, or the prototype of the fourth root-race, works in close co-operation with Him, and has His centre of influence in China.

He is the second Manu that the fourth root-race has had, having taken the place of the earlier Manu at the time of the final stages of Atlantean destruction. He has remained to foster the development of the race type, and to bring about its final disappearance. The periods of office of all the Manus overlap, but there remains no representative of the third root-race upon the globe at this time. Vaivasvata Manu has His dwelling place in the Himalaya mountains, and has gathered around Him at Shigatse some of those immediately connected with Aryan affairs in India, Europe and America, and those who will later be concerned with the coming sixth root-race.

The plans are prepared for ages ahead, centres of energy are formed thousands of years before they will be required, and in the wise fore-knowledge of these Divine Men nothing is left to sudden eventuation, but all moves in ordered cycles and under rule and law, though within karmic limitations.

The work of the Manu is largely concerned with government, with planetary politics, and with the founding, direction, and dissolution of racial types and forms. To Him is committed the will and purpose of the Planetary Logos. He knows what is the immediate objective for this cycle of evolution over which He has to preside, and His work concerns itself with making that will an accomplished fact.

He works in closer co-operation with the building devas than does His Brother, the Christ, for to Him is given the work of setting the race type, of segregating the groups out of which races will develop, of manipulating the forces which move the earth's crust, of raising and lowering continents, of directing the minds of statesmen everywhere so that racial government will proceed as desired, and conditions be brought about which will produce those needed for the fostering of any particular type. Such a work can now be seen demonstrating in North America and Australia.

The energy which flows through Him emanates from the head centre of the Planetary Logos, passing to Him through the brain of Sanat Kumara, Who focalizes all the planetary energy within Himself. He works by the means of a dynamic meditation, conducted within the head centre, and produces His results through His perfect realization of that which has to be accomplished, through a power to visualize that which must be done to bring about accomplishment, and through a capacity to transmit creative and destructive energy to those who are His assistants. And all this is brought about through the power of the enunciated sound.

The work of the World Teacher, the Christ

Group two has the World Teacher for its presiding Head. He is that Great Being Whom the Christian calls the Christ; He is known also in the Orient as the Bodhisattva, and as the Lord Maitreya, and is the One looked for by the devout Mohammedan, under the name of the Iman Madhi. He it is Who has presided over the destinies of life since about 600 B.C. and He it is Who has come out among men before, and Who is again looked for. He is the great Lord of Love and of

Compassion, just as his predecessor, the Buddha, was the Lord of Wisdom. Through Him flows the energy of the second aspect, reaching Him direct from the heart centre of the Planetary Logos via the heart of Sanat Kumara. He works by means of a meditation centered within the heart. He is the World Teacher, the Master of the Masters, and the Instructor of the Angels, and to Him is committed the guidance of the spiritual destinies of men, and the development of the realization within each human being that he is a child of God and a son of the Most High.

Just as the Manu is occupied with the providing of the type and forms through which consciousness can evolve and gather experience, thus making existence in its deepest sense possible, so the World Teacher directs that indwelling consciousness in its life or spirit aspect, seeking to energize it within the form so that, in due course of time, that form can be discarded and the liberated spirit return whence it came.

Ever since He left the earth, as related with approximate accuracy in the Bible story (though with much error in detail) has He stayed with the sons of men; never has He really gone, but only in appearance, and in a physical body He can be found by those who know the way, dwelling in the Himalayas, and working in close co-operation with His two great Brothers, the Manu and the Mahachohan. Daily He pours out His blessing on the world, and daily He stands under the great pine in His garden at the sunset hour with hands uplifted in blessing over all those who truly and earnestly seek to aspire.

To Him all seekers are known, and, though they may remain unaware of Him, the light which He pours forth stimulates their desire, fosters the spark of struggling life and spurs on the aspirant until the momentous day dawns when they stand face to face with the One Who by being "lifted up" (occultly understood) is drawing all men unto Himself as the Initiator of the sacred mysteries.

The work of the Lord of Civilization, the Mahachohan

Group three has as its Head the Mahachohan. His rule over the group persists for a longer period than that of His two Brothers, and He may hold office for the term of several root-races. He is the sum-total of the intelligence aspect. The present Mahachohan is not the original one Who held the office at the founding of the Hierarchy in Lemurian days—it was then held by one of the Kumaras, or Lords of the Flame, Who came into incarnation with Sanat Kumara—but He took hold of His position during the second sub-race of the Atlantean root-race.

He had achieved adept-ship on the moon-chain, and it was through His instrumentality that a large number of the present more advanced human beings came into incarnation in the middle of the Atlantean root-race. Karmic affiliation with Him was one of the predisposing causes, thus making this eventuality possible.

His work concerns itself with the fostering and strengthening of that relation between spirit and matter, life and form, the self and the not-self, which results in what we call civilization. He manipulates the forces of nature, and is largely the emanating source of electrical energy as we know it. Being the reflection of the third, or creative aspect, energy from the Planetary Logos flows to Him from the throat centre, and He it is Who in many ways makes the work of His Brothers possible. Their plans and desires are submitted to Him, and through Him pass the instructions to a large number of the deva agents.

Thus you have Will, Love, and Intelligence represented in these three great Lords; you have the self, the not-self, and the relation between synthesized in the unity of manifestation; you have racial government, religion and civilization forming a coherent whole, and you have physical manifestation, the love or desire aspect, and the mind of the Planetary Logos working out into objectivity. The closest co-operation and unity exists between these three Personalities, and every move and plan and event exists in Their united foreknowledge. They are in daily touch with the Lord of the World at Shamballa, and the entire guidance of affairs rests in Their hands, and in those of the Manu of the fourth root-race. The World Teacher holds office in connection with both the fourth and fifth root-races.

Each of these departmental heads directs a number of subsidiary offices, and the department of the Mahachohan is divided into five divisions, so as to take in the four lesser aspects of Hierarchical rule.

Under the Manu work the regents of the different world divisions, such as, for instance, the Master Jupiter, the oldest of the Masters now working in physical bodies for humanity, Who is the regent for India, and the Master Rakoczi, Who is the regent for Europe and America. It must be remembered here that though the Master R., for instance, belongs to the seventh ray, and thus comes under the department of energy of the Mahachohan, yet in Hierarchical work He may and does hold office temporarily under the Manu.

These regents hold in Their hands the reins of government for continents and nations, thus guiding, even if unknown, their destinies; They impress and inspire statesmen and rulers; They pour forth mental energy on governing groups, thus bringing about the desired results wherever co-operation and receptive intuition can be found amongst the thinkers.

The World Teacher presides over the destiny of the great religions through the medium of a group of Masters and initiates Who direct the activities of these different schools of thought. In illustration:—The Master Jesus, the inspirer and director of the Christian Churches everywhere, though an adept on the sixth ray under the department of the Mahachohan, works at present under the Christ for the welfare of Christianity; other Masters hold similar posts in relation to the great oriental faiths, and the various occidental schools of thought.

In the department of the Mahachohan a large number of Masters, in fivefold division, work in connection with the deva evolution, and with the intelligence aspect in man.

Their divisions follow those of the four minor rays of attribute:—
1. The ray of harmony or beauty.
2. The ray of concrete science or knowledge.
3. The ray of devotion or abstract idealism.
4. The ray of ceremonial law or magic,

just as the three departmental heads represent the three major rays of:—
I.   Will or power.

II.   Love or wisdom.
III. Active intelligence, or adaptability.

The four rays or attributes of mind, with the third ray of intelligence, as synthesized by the Mahachohan, make up the sum-total of the fifth principle of mind or manas.

THE DEPARTMENTAL HEADS.

The Manu.

The Bodhisattva.

The Mahachohan.

As has been said, these three great Beings represent the triplicity of all manifestation, and might be expressed under the following form, remembering that all this deals with subjectivity, and therefore with the evolution of consciousness and primarily with self-consciousness in man.

Consciousness

The Manu. The Bodhisattva   The Mahachohan

Matter aspect.....Spirit aspect .... Intelligence
aspect.

Form ....
Life .... Mind.

The Not-Self .... The
Self .... The relation between.

Body ....
Spirit .... Soul.

Or, in words strictly dealing with self-conscious
realization,

Politics................................
Religion................................ Science.

Government..........................
Beliefs................................... Civilization.

Races...................................
Faiths................................... Education.

All human beings belong to one or other of these three departments, and all are of equal importance, for Spirit and matter are one. All are so interdependent, being but expressions of one life, that the endeavour to express the functions of the three departments in tabular form is liable to lead to error.

The three Great Lords closely co-operate in the work, and that work is one, just as man, though a triplicity, is yet an individual unit. The human being is a form through which a spiritual life or entity is manifesting, and employing the intelligence under evolutionary law.

Therefore the Great Lords are closely connected with the initiations of a human unit. They are too occupied with greater affairs and with group activities to have any relationship with a man until he stands upon the probationary path. When he has, through his own effort, brought himself on to the Path of Discipleship, the particular Master Who has him under supervision reports to the head of one of the three departments (this being dependent upon a man's ray) that he is nearing the Portal of Initiation and should be ready for the great step during such and such a life. Each life, and later each year, report is made, until the final year upon the Path of Probation, when closer and more frequent reports are handed in. During this final year also, the applicant's name is submitted to the Lodge, and after his own Master has reported upon him, and his record has been briefly summarized, his name is balloted, and sponsors are arranged.

During the initiation ceremony the important factors are:
—

1. The Initiator.

2. The triangle of force formed by three adepts or three Kumaras.

3. The sponsors.

In the case of the first two initiations, two Masters stand, one on each side of the applicant, within the triangle; at the third, fourth and fifth initiations, the Mahachohan and the Bodhisattva perform the function of sponsor; at the sixth and seventh initiations two great Beings, Who must remain nameless, stand within the esoteric triangle. The work of the sponsors is to pass through Their bodies the force or electrical energy emanating from the Rod of Initiation. This force, through radiation, circles around the triangle and is supplemented by the force of the three guardians; it next passes through the centers of the sponsors, being transmitted by an act of will to the initiate.

Enough has been said elsewhere in this book anent the Lodge of Masters and Their relation to the applicant for Initiation, whilst the work of the initiate himself has been likewise touched upon. That work is not unknown to the children of men everywhere, but remains as yet an ideal and a far-off possibility. Yet when a man strives to reach that ideal, to make it a demonstrating fact within himself, he will find that it becomes not only a possibility, but something attainable, provided he strives sufficiently. The first initiation is within the reach of many, but the necessary one-pointedness and the firm belief in the reality ahead, coupled to a willingness to sacrifice all rather than turn back, are deterrents to the many. If this book serves no other purpose than to spur some one to renewed believing effort, it will not have been written in vain.

Initiation, Human and Solar
A.A.B.

A Contemporary Expansion on the Three Departments of Hierarchy

Having now explored the sacred words of the Tibetan Master through Alice A. Bailey's transmission, let us step back into the present moment to weave these truths into our modern framework of understanding. The world today stands in a crucible of transformation. What once was hidden now longs to be known. The Inner Government of the World—*the Planetary Hierarchy*—is not merely a spiritual ideal, but the living foundation of planetary evolution. Its structure, so elegantly described in the teachings of A.A.B., remains unchanged in essence but increasingly accessible to those with awakened hearts and trained minds.

It may serve the seeker well to recognize that the **three departments** of the Hierarchy are not rigid bureaucracies. They are **currents of Divine Will**—living emanations of spiritual energy that operate within precise laws and rhythms. These departments are as alive and intelligent as the human beings they seek to serve, and their energy infuses our world through subtle and not-so-subtle means: movements, revolutions, reforms, scientific breakthroughs, cultural renaissances, and awakenings of faith.

Let us speak now, in modern terms, of what these three departments *mean* for us.

The Manu and the Department of Divine Government

The Department of the Manu is responsible for shaping the destiny of races, nations, and continents. It works with great cycles of time, over thousands of years, and concerns itself with the *outer forms* through which the soul of humanity expresses. In our era, this department is overseeing a major karmic recalibration—the **restructuring of global power**, the dissolution of outdated national identities, and the seeding of future racial types that are more attuned to the soul's vibration.

To recognize the hand of the Manu is to see the **hidden order in global disruption**. Every migration, every collapse of empire, every shift in demographics and culture is being guided—albeit indirectly—by this department. The rise of global consciousness and planetary identity is part of the Manu's great Work. Those drawn to politics, law, justice, or humanitarian restructuring are often unknowingly responding to this first ray current.

As White Magic gives way to Agni Yoga, those aligned with the Department of the Manu must learn to become channels of **right will** rather than personal ambition. Their task is not to control but to *hold the pattern*, to invoke order through service, and to build the new civilizations that will house the evolving soul of humanity.

The Christ and the Department of Love-Wisdom

The second department, under the World Teacher, is the most accessible to the heart of humanity. The Lord Maitreya—the Christ—anchors this energy, and His influence is streaming more powerfully than ever into the human family.

Here we are dealing not only with religion, but with **consciousness itself**—its refinement, elevation, and unification. The religions of the past, though often distorted by doctrine and politics, were born from this source. Today, this department calls not for more division, but for **universal synthesis**—the weaving together of diverse traditions into the shared realization that Love is Law, and Law is Love.

This energy touches all forms of **education, healing, spiritual practice, and collective empathy**. Artists, counselors, mystics, holistic doctors, and interfaith leaders —all those working to uplift the emotional and mental bodies of humanity—are often aligned with this ray. The Christ does not demand worship; He calls for embodiment. Those who magnetize others with their calm presence, compassion, and integrity are His emissaries.

And for the modern disciple, the challenge is to move beyond emotional devotion into **radiatory service**—to become transmitters of love-wisdom in action, even when no one is watching.

The Mahachohan and the Department of Creative Intelligence

The third department is perhaps the most misunderstood, yet increasingly crucial in our age of technology and mass communication. The Mahachohan governs the outpouring of **ceremonial order, science, philosophy, and the arts**. It is here that the sub-rays (rays 4–7) are synthesized and distributed.

This is the **department of the world's thinkers, scientists, inventors, technologists, ritualists, and innovators**. It is also where the danger of misused intelligence is most acute. The distortion of truth, the weaponization of science, and the glamorization of materialism are shadows of this ray.

But it is also where **the fusion of occultism and science** will take root. The true esoteric scientist, the ceremonial magician in service to the Plan, the sacred technologist of the Aquarian Age—these are the vehicles for the Mahachohan's will. As the veil thins, we will see more collaboration between scientific and spiritual communities. That is inevitable.

For the disciple aligned with this ray, the work is to **refine the mind**, but not to worship it. One must become a knower who remembers to feel, a ritualist who remembers to serve, a thinker who remembers to pray.

The Three Become One: The Synthesis of Rays and the Emergence of the New Humanity

These three departments are never in competition. They function in **perfect harmonic resonance**, just as the three aspects of a single human being—body, soul, and spirit—are meant to function. In truth, no disciple works with only one department. Though your primary soul ray aligns you more directly with one, your path of initiation eventually brings you into **right relationship with all three**.

The Hierarchy is not interested in your personality's career or spiritual brand. It is interested in your ability to become a **focal point of the Plan**, to wield power harmlessly, love impersonally, and think clearly. Those who do so become living bridges between Shamballa and humanity—**agents of planetary transfiguration**.

Let this be understood: The Hierarchy is not a myth or metaphor. It is real. It is watching. It is guiding. And it is preparing to **externalize**—to walk again among humanity in forms both subtle and tangible. But it cannot descend fully until we have raised ourselves to meet it halfway.

That is the work. That is the call. And that is why you are here.

Let us now continue this sacred dialogue, walking step by step through the architecture of the Hierarchy, so that we might begin to recognize its influence—not just in books or scriptures, but in our very lives.

The Ashrams and the Living Body of the Hierarchy

It is now time to deepen our understanding of the Hierarchy by exploring one of its most intimate expressions: the **Ashrams of the Masters**. If the three departments are the broad arteries through which divine energy flows into human evolution, then the Ashrams are the **living organs of spiritual transmission**, each structured around a Master who serves as both teacher and radiatory point of the Divine Will.

An Ashram is not a building. It is a **sphere of influence**, a magnetic field composed of aligned Souls—disciples, initiates, and sometimes advanced aspirants—who have become group-conscious and soul-infused. These Ashrams exist on the higher mental plane and extend into the causal bodies of those linked with their vibratory tone. They do not exist in isolation but radiate energy **directly into the world** through the thoughts, choices, and actions of their members.

Each Ashram is built around a **Ray**—a specific frequency of divine purpose. There are seven primary ashrams corresponding to the seven rays, all organized under the three major departments. The ashrams are directed by Masters, or Chohans, who themselves are expressions of perfected consciousness working directly with the Will of the Planetary Logos. These Masters were once human and have now moved beyond the cycle of ordinary reincarnation.

For example:

- The **First Ray Ashram**, under the Department of the Manu, radiates the **energy of Will and Power**, and is often led by Masters like El Morya. Its members include those who are destined to wield influence over policy, leadership, and the structuring of human institutions.

- The **Second Ray Ashram**, under the Christ, expresses **Love-Wisdom** and is led by Masters such as Kuthumi. It draws those in education, healing, and spiritual ministry.

- The **Third Ray Ashram**, under the Mahachohan, is the fountainhead of **Active Intelligence**, attracting thinkers, inventors, and those destined to reshape civilization itself.

Every disciple belongs to one of these rays, though over the course of their spiritual evolution, they will learn to work in harmony with all seven.

These ashrams are **not static**. They evolve in response to humanity's needs. New sub-ashrams are forming, particularly in this transition into the Aquarian Age. Some disciples today are aligned with Ashrams whose Masters have not yet externalized, but whose energy is preparing to manifest through groups in art, science, governance, and ecological stewardship.

It is essential for seekers to remember: an Ashram is **not joined by application or request**. It is joined by **vibration and resonance**. When one's soul reaches a sufficient frequency of purity, discipline, and loving service, a line of energy will form between the aspirant and the ashramic field. This is often the first signal that one is approaching the **Path of Accepted Discipleship**.

Disciples within an Ashram are expected to eventually become **radiatory centers**—clear channels through which the purpose of the Ashram flows unimpeded. It is in this capacity that they help transmit new ideas, uplift humanity, and embody the sacred principles of the Plan in ordinary life. Some serve in silence, others teach, some write or heal or lead—but all, in their own way, become part of the **backbone of spiritual civilization**.

The Ashrams are the **limbs and fingers of Hierarchy**. They reach into the world through you.

Let this section serve as an invitation—not just to admire or believe in the Ashrams, but to prepare yourself to eventually become *one of them*. Study the rays. Meditate with precision. Live with harmlessness and devotion. Serve with strength and grace. Let your daily life become the preparation ground for contact with the inner Ashram to which your Soul is aligned.

The door is not locked. But only those who walk in humility, perseverance, and love will find it open.

W.M.A.

THE WORK OF THE HIERARCHY

Though the subject of the occult Hierarchy of the planet is of such a profoundly momentous interest to the average man, yet its real significance will never be understood until men realize three things in connection with it.   First, that the entire Hierarchy of spiritual beings represents a synthesis of forces or of energies, which forces or energies are consciously manipulated for the furtherance of planetary evolution.   This will become more apparent as we proceed.   Secondly, that these forces, demonstrating in our planetary scheme through those great Personalities Who compose the Hierarchy, link it and all that it contains with the greater Hierarchy which we call Solar.   Our Hierarchy is a miniature replica of the greater synthesis of those self-conscious Entities who manipulate, control, and demonstrate through the sun and the seven sacred planets, as well as the other planets, greater and smaller, of which our solar system is composed.   Thirdly, that this Hierarchy of forces has four pre-eminent lines of work:—

TO DEVELOP SELF-CONSCIOUSNESS IN ALL BEINGS.

The Hierarchy seeks to provide fit conditions for the development of self-consciousness in all beings.   This it produces primarily in man through its initial work of blending the higher three aspects of spirit with the lower four; through the example it sets of service, sacrifice, and renunciation, and through the constant streams of light (occultly understood) which emanate from it.   The

Hierarchy might be considered as the aggregate on our planet of the forces of the fifth kingdom in nature. This kingdom is entered through the full development and control of the fifth principle of mind, and its transmutation into wisdom, which is literally the intelligence applied to all states through the full conscious utilisation of the faculty of discriminative love.

TO DEVELOP CONSCIOUSNESS IN THE THREE LOWER KINGDOMS.

As is well known, the five kingdoms of nature on the evolutionary arc might be defined as follows:—the mineral kingdom, the vegetable kingdom, the animal kingdom, the human kingdom, and the spiritual kingdom. All these kingdoms embody some type of consciousness, and it is the work of the Hierarchy to develop these types to perfection through the adjustment of karma, through the agency of force, and through the providing of right conditions. Some idea of the work may be gained if we briefly summarize the different aspects of consciousness to be developed in the various kingdoms.

In the *mineral kingdom* the work of the Hierarchy is directed toward the development of the discriminative and selective activity. One characteristic of all matter is activity of some kind, and the moment that activity is directed towards the building of forms, even of the most elemental kind, the faculty of discrimination will demonstrate. This is recognised by scientists everywhere, and in this recognition, they are approximating the findings of the Divine Wisdom.

In the *vegetable kingdom*, to this faculty of discrimination is added that of response to sensation, and the rudimentary condition of the second aspect of divinity is to be seen, just as in the mineral kingdom a similar rudimentary reflection of the third aspect of activity is making itself felt.

In the *animal kingdom* this rudimentary activity and feeling are increased, and symptoms (if it might be so inadequately expressed) are to be found of the first aspect, or embryonic will and purpose; we may call it hereditary instinct, but it works out in fact as purpose in nature.

It has been wisely stated by H. P. Blavatsky that man is the macrocosm for the three lower kingdoms, for in him these three lines of development are synthesized and come to their full fruition. He is verily and indeed intelligence, actively and wonderfully manifested; He is incipient love and wisdom, even though as yet they may be but the goal of his endeavour; and he has that embryonic, dynamic, initiating will which will come to a fuller development after he has entered into the fifth kingdom.

In the fifth kingdom, the consciousness to be developed is that of the group, and this shows itself in the full flowering of the love-wisdom faculty. Man but repeats on a higher turn of the spiral, the work of the three lower kingdoms, for in the human kingdom he shows forth the third aspect of active intelligence. In the fifth kingdom, which is entered at the first initiation, and which covers all the period of time wherein a man takes the first five initiations, and that wherein he works as a Master, as part of the Hierarchy, the love-wisdom, or second aspect, comes to its consummation.

At the sixth and seventh initiations the first, or will, aspect shines forth, and from being a Master of Compassion and a Lord of Love the adept becomes something more. He enters into a still higher consciousness than that of the group, and becomes God-conscious. The great will or purpose of the Logos becomes his.

The fostering of the various attributes of divinity, the tending of the seed of self-consciousness in all beings, is the work of those Entities who have achieved, Who have entered into the fifth kingdom and Who have there made Their great decision, and that inconceivable renunciation which leads Them to stay within the planetary scheme, and thus co-operate with the plans of the Planetary Logos on the physical plane.

TO TRANSMIT THE WILL OF THE PLANETARY LOGOS

They act as the transmitter to men and devas or angels, of the will of the Planetary Logos, and through Him of the Solar Logos. Each planetary scheme, ours amongst the others, is a centre in the body Logoic, and is expressing some form of energy or force. Each centre expresses its particular type of force, demonstrated in a triple manner, producing thus universally the three aspects in manifestation. One of the great realizations which come to those who enter into the fifth kingdom is that of the particular type of force which our own Planetary Logos embodies.

The wise student will ponder on this statement, for it holds the clue to much that may be seen in the world today. The secret of synthesis has been lost, and only when men again get back the knowledge which was theirs in earlier cycles (having been mercifully withdrawn in Atlantean days) of the type of energy which our scheme should be demonstrating, will the world problems adjust themselves, and the world rhythm be stabilized.

This cannot be as yet, for this knowledge is of a dangerous kind, and at present the race as a whole is not group conscious, and therefore cannot be trusted to work, think, plan, and act for the group. Man is as yet too selfish, but there is no cause for discouragement in this fact; group consciousness is already somewhat more than a vision, whilst brotherhood, and the recognition of its obligations, is beginning to permeate the consciousness of men everywhere. This is the work of the Hierarchy of Light,— to demonstrate to men the true meaning of brotherhood, and to foster in them response to that ideal which is latent in one and all.

TO SET AN EXAMPLE TO HUMANITY.

The fourth thing that men need to know and to realize as a basic fact is that this Hierarchy is composed of those Who have triumphed over matter, and Who have achieved the goal by the very self-same steps that individuals tread today. These spiritual personalities, these adepts and Masters, have wrestled and fought for victory and mastery upon the physical plane, and struggled with the miasmas, the fogs, the dangers, the troubles, the sorrows and pains of everyday living.

They have trodden every step of the path of suffering, have undergone every experience, have surmounted every difficulty, and have won out. These Elder Brothers of the race have one and all undergone the crucifixion of the personal self, and know that utter renunciation of all which is the lot of every aspirant at this time. There is no phase of agony, no rending sacrifice, no Via Dolorosa that They have not in Their time trodden, and herein lies Their right to serve, and the strength of the method of Their appeal.

Knowing the quintessence of pain, knowing the depth of sin and of suffering, Their methods can be exquisitely measured to the individual need; yet at the same time Their realization of the liberation to be achieved through pain, penalty, and suffering, and Their apprehension of the freedom that comes through the sacrifice of the form by the medium of the purificatory fires, suffices to give Them a firm hand, an ability to persist even when the form may seem to have undergone a sufficiency of suffering, and a love that triumphs over all setbacks, for it is founded on patience and experience.

These Elder Brothers of humanity are characterized by a *love* which endures, and which acts ever for the good of the group; by a *knowledge* which has been gained through millennia of lives, in which They have worked Their way from the bottom of life and of evolution well nigh to the top; by an *experience* which is based on time itself and a multiplicity of personality reactions and interactions; by a *courage* which is the result of that experience, and which, having itself been produced by ages of endeavour, failure, and renewed endeavour, and having in the long run led to triumph, can now be placed at the service of the race; by a *purpose* which is enlightened and intelligent, and which is co-operative, adjusting itself to the group and hierarchical plan and thus fitting in with the purpose of the Planetary Logos; and finally They are distinguished by a knowledge of the *power of sound*.

This final fact is the basis of that aphorism which states that all true occultists are distinguished by the characteristics of knowledge, dynamic will, courage, and silence. "To know, to will, to dare, and to be silent." Knowing the plan so well, and having clear, illuminated vision, They can bend Their will unflinchingly and unswervingly to the great work of creation by the power of sound. This leads to Their silence where the average man would speak, and Their speaking where the average man is silent.

When men have grasped the four facts here enumerated, and they are established as acknowledged truths in the consciousness of the race, then may we look for a return of that cycle of peace and rest and righteousness which is foretold in all the Scriptures of the world. The Sun of Righteousness will then arise with healing in His wings, and the peace which passeth understanding will reign in the hearts of men.

In dealing with this matter of the work of the occult Hierarchy, in a book for the general public, much must be left unsaid. The average man is interested and his curiosity is aroused by reference to these Personalities, but men are not yet ready for more than the most general information. For those who, from curiosity, pass on to desire and seek to know the truth as it is, more will be forthcoming, when they themselves have done the necessary work and study. Investigation is desired, and the attitude of mind which it is hoped this book will arouse might be summed up in the following words:— These statements sound interesting and perchance they are true. The religions of all nations, the Christian included, give indications that seem to substantiate these ideas. Let us therefore accept these ideas as a working hypothesis as to the consummation of the evolutionary process in man and his work upon the attainment of perfection.

Let us therefore seek for the truth as a fact in our own consciousness. Every religious faith holds out the promise that those who seek with earnestness shall find that which they are seeking; let us, therefore, seek. If by our search we find that all these statements are but visionary dreams, and profit not at all, leading us only into darkness, time will nevertheless not have been lost, for we shall have ascertained where not to look. If by our search, on the other hand, corroboration comes little by little, and the light shines ever more clearly, let us persist until that day dawns when the light which shineth in darkness will have illuminated the heart and brain, and the seeker will awaken to the realization that the whole trend of evolution has been to bring him this expansion of consciousness and this illumination, and that the attainment of the initiatory process, and the entrance into the fifth kingdom is no wild chimera or phantasm, but an established fact in the consciousness.

This each man must ascertain for himself. Those who know may state a fact to be thus and so, but the dictum of another person and the enunciation of a theory do not aid beyond giving to the seeker confirmatory indication. Each soul has to ascertain for himself, and must find out within himself, remembering ever that the kingdom of God is within, and that only those facts which are realized within the individual consciousness as truths are of any real value. In the meantime, that which many know, and have ascertained within themselves to be truths of an incontrovertible nature for them, may here be stated; to the intelligent reader will then arise the opportunity and the responsibility of ascertaining for himself their falsity or truth.

THE FOUNDING OF THE HIERARCHY
ITS APPEARANCE ON THE PLANET.

It is not sought, in this book, to deal with the steps which led to the founding of the Hierarchy on the planet, nor to consider the conditions preceding the advent of those great Beings. This can be studied in other occult books in the occident, and in the sacred Scriptures of the East. Suffice it for our purpose to say that in the middle of the Lemurian epoch, approximately eighteen million years ago, occurred a great event which signified, among other things, the following developments:—The Planetary Logos of our earth scheme, one of the Seven Spirits before the throne, took physical incarnation, and, under the form of Sanat Kumara, the Ancient of Days, and the Lord of the World, came down to this dense physical planet and has remained with us ever since.

Owing to the extreme purity of His nature, and the fact that He is (from the human standpoint) relatively sinless, and hence incapable of response to aught on the dense physical plane, He was unable to take a dense physical body such as ours, and has to function in His etheric body. He is the greatest of all the Avatars, or Coming Ones, for He is a direct reflection of that great Entity who lives, and breathes, and functions through all the evolutions on this planet, holding all within His aura or magnetic sphere of influence.

In Him we live and move and have our being, and none of us can pass beyond the radius of His aura. He is the Great Sacrifice, Who left the glory of the high places and for the sake of the evolving sons of men took upon Himself a

physical form and was made in the likeness of man. He is
the Silent Watcher, as far as our immediate humanity is
concerned, although literally the Planetary Logos Himself,
on the higher plane of consciousness whereon He
functions, is the true Silent Watcher where the planetary
scheme is concerned.

Perhaps it might be stated thus:—That the Lord of the
World, the One Initiator, holds the same place in
connection with the Planetary Logos as the physical
manifestation of a Master holds to that Master's Monad on
the monadic plane. In both cases the intermediate state of
consciousness has been superseded, that of the Ego or
higher self, and that which we see and know is the *direct*
self-created manifestation of pure spirit itself. Hence the
sacrifice.

It must here be borne in mind that in the case of Sanat
Kumara there is a tremendous difference in degree, for His
point in evolution is as far in advance of that of an adept
as that adept's is in advance of animal man. This will be
somewhat elaborated in the next section of our subject.

With the Ancient of Days came a group of other highly
evolved Entities, who represent His own individual karmic
group and those Beings who are the outcome of the triple
nature of the Planetary Logos. If one might so express it
They embody the forces emanating from the head, heart,
and throat centres, and They came in with Sanat Kumara
to form focal points of planetary force for the helping of
the great plan for the self-conscious unfoldment of all
life.

Their places have gradually been filled by the sons of men as they qualify, though this includes very few, until lately, from our immediate earth humanity. Those who are now the inner group around the Lord of the World have been primarily recruited from the ranks of those who were initiates on the moon chain (the cycle of evolution [30] preceding ours) or who have come in on certain streams of solar energy, astrologically determined, from other planetary schemes, yet those who have triumphed in our own humanity are rapidly increasing in number, and hold all the minor offices beneath the central esoteric group of Six, who, with the Lord of the World, form the heart of hierarchical effort.

THE IMMEDIATE EFFECT.

The result of Their advent, millions of years ago, was stupendous, and its effects are still being felt. Those effects might be enumerated as follows:—The Planetary Logos on His own plane was enabled to take a more direct method in producing the results He desired for working out His plan.

As is well known, the planetary scheme, with its dense globe and inner subtler globes, is to the Planetary Logos what the physical body and its subtler bodies are to man. Hence in illustration it might be said that the coming into incarnation of Sanat Kumara was analogous to the firm grip of self-conscious control that the Ego of a human being takes upon his vehicles when the necessary stage in evolution has been achieved.

It has been said that in the head of every man are seven centres of force, which are linked to the other centres in the body, and through which the force of the Ego is spread and circulated, thus working out the plan. Sanat Kumara, with the six other Kumaras, holds a similar position. These central seven are as the seven head centres to the body corporate.

They are the directing agents and the transmitters of the energy, force, purpose, and will of the Planetary Logos on His own plane. This planetary head centre works directly through the heart and throat centres, and thereby controls all the remaining centres. This is by way of illustration, and an attempt to show the relation of the Hierarchy to its planetary source, and also the close analogy between the method of functioning of a Planetary Logos and of man, the microcosm.

The third kingdom of nature, the animal kingdom, had reached a relatively high state of evolution, and animal man was in possession of the earth; he was a being with a powerful physical body, a co-ordinated astral body, or body of sensation and feeling, and a rudimentary germ of mind which might some day form a nucleus of a mental body.

Left to himself for long aeons animal man would have eventually progressed out of the animal kingdom into the human, and would have become a self-conscious, functioning, rational entity, but how slow the process would have been may be evidenced by the study of the bushmen of South Africa, the Veddhas of Ceylon, and the hairy Ainus.

The decision of the Planetary Logos to take a physical vehicle produced an extraordinary stimulation in the evolutionary process, and by His incarnation, and the methods of force distribution He employed, He brought about in a brief cycle of time what would otherwise have been inconceivably slow.   The germ of mind in animal man was stimulated.

The fourfold lower man,

a. The physical body in its dual capacity, etheric and dense,
b. Vitality, life force, or prana,
c. The astral or emotional body,
d. The incipient germ of mind,

was co-ordinated and stimulated, and became a fit receptacle for the coming in of the self-conscious entities, those spiritual triads (the reflection of spiritual will, intuition, or wisdom, and higher mind) who had for long ages been waiting for just such a fitting.   The fourth, or human kingdom, came thus into being, and the self-conscious, or rational unit, man, began his career.
Another result of the advent of the Hierarchy was a similar, though less recognized development in all the kingdoms of nature.

In the mineral kingdom, for instance, certain of the minerals or elements received an added stimulation, and became radioactive, and a mysterious chemical change took place in the vegetable kingdom. This facilitated the bridging process between the vegetable and animal kingdoms, just as the radio-activity of minerals is the method of bridging the gulf between the mineral and vegetable kingdoms.

In due course of time scientists will recognize that every kingdom in nature is linked and entered when the units of that kingdom become radioactive. But it is not necessary for us to digress along these lines. A hint suffices for those who have eyes to see, and the intuition to comprehend the meaning conveyed by terms which are handicapped by having a purely material connotation.

In Lemurian days, after the great descent of the spiritual Existences to the earth, the work They planned to do was systematized. Offices were apportioned, and the processes of evolution in all the departments of nature were brought under the conscious wise guidance of this initial Brotherhood. This Hierarchy of Brothers of Light still exists, and the work goes steadily on.

They are all in physical existence, either in dense physical bodies, such as many of the Masters employ, or in etheric bodies, such as the more exalted helpers and the Lord of the World occupy. It is of value for men to remember that They are in physical existence, and to bear in mind that They exist upon this planet with us, controlling its destinies, guiding its affairs, and leading all its evolutions on to an ultimate perfection.

The central home of this Hierarchy is at Shamballa, a centre in the Gobi desert, called in the ancient books the "White Island." It exists in etheric matter, and when the race of men on earth have developed etheric vision its location will be recognized and its reality admitted. The development of this vision is rapidly coming to pass, as may be seen from the newspapers and the current literature of the day, but the location of Shamballa will be one of the latest etheric sacred spots to be revealed as it exists in the matter of the second ether.

Several of the Masters in physical bodies dwell in the Himalaya mountains, in a secluded spot called Shigatse, far from the ways of men, but the greater number are scattered all over the world, dwelling in different places in the various nations, unrecognized and unknown, yet forming each in His own place a focal point for the energy of the Lord of the World, and proving to His environment a distributor of the love and wisdom of the Deity.

THE OPENING OF THE DOOR OF INITIATION.

It is not possible to touch upon the history of the Hierarchy during the long ages of its work, beyond mentioning certain outstanding events of the past, and pointing out certain eventualities. For ages after its immediate founding, the work was slow and discouraging.

Thousands of years came and went, and races of men appeared and disappeared from the earth before it was possible to delegate even the work done by initiates of the first degree to the evolving sons of men. But in the middle of the fourth root-race, the Atlantean, an event occurred which necessitated a change, or innovation in the Hierarchical method. Certain of its members were called away to higher work elsewhere in the solar system, and this brought in, through necessity, a number of highly evolved units of the human family.

In order to enable others to take Their place, the lesser members of the Hierarchy were all moved up a step, leaving vacancies among the minor posts. Therefore three things were decided upon in the Council Chamber of the Lord of the World.

1. To close the door through which animal men passed into the human kingdom, permitting for a time no more Monads on the higher plane to appropriate bodies. This restricted the number of the fourth, or human kingdom, to its then limitation.

2. To open another door, and permit members of the human family who were willing to undergo the necessary discipline and to make the required stupendous effort, to enter the fifth or spiritual kingdom. In this way the ranks of the Hierarchy could be filled by the members of earth's humanity who qualified. This door is called the Portal of Initiation, and still remains open upon the same terms as laid down by the Lord of the World in Atlantean days. These terms will be stated in the last chapter of this book. The door between the human and animal kingdoms will again be opened during the next great cycle, or "round" as it is called in some books, but as this is several million years away from us at this time, we are not concerned with it.

3. It was also decided to make the line of demarcation between the two forces of matter and spirit clearly defined; the inherent duality of all manifestation was

emphasized, with the aim in view of teaching men who want to liberate themselves from the limitations of the fourth, or human kingdom, and thus pass on into the fifth, or spiritual.

The problem of good or evil, light or darkness, right or wrong, was enunciated solely for the benefit of humanity, and to enable men to cast off the fetters which imprisoned spirit, and thus achieve spiritual freedom. This problem exists not in the kingdoms below man, nor for those who transcend the human. Man has to learn through experience and pain the fact of the duality of all existence.

Having thus learnt, he chooses that which concerns the fully conscious spirit aspect of divinity, and learns to centre himself in that aspect. Having thus achieved liberation he finds indeed that all is one, that spirit and matter are a unity, naught existing save that which is to be found within the consciousness of the Planetary Logos, and—in wider circles—within the consciousness of the Solar Logos.

The Hierarchy thus took advantage of the discriminative faculty of mind, which is the distinctive quality of humanity, to enable him, through the balancing of the pairs of opposites, to reach his goal, and to find his way back to the source from whence he came.

This decision led to that great struggle which distinguished the Atlantean civilization, and which culminated in the destruction called the flood, referred to in all the Scriptures of the world. The forces of light, and the forces of darkness, were arrayed against each other, and this for the helping of humanity. The struggle still persists, and the World War through which we have just passed was a recrudescence of it. On every side in that World War two groups were to be found, those who fought for an ideal as they saw it, for the highest that they knew, and those who fought for material and selfish advantage. In the struggle of these influential idealists or materialists many were swept in who fought blindly and ignorantly, being thus overwhelmed with racial karma and disaster.

These three decisions of the Hierarchy are having, and will have a profound effect upon humanity, but the result desired is being achieved, and a rapid hastening of the evolutionary process, and a profoundly important effect upon the mind aspect in man, can already be seen.

It might here be well to point out that, working as members of that Hierarchy are a great number of beings called angels by the Christian, and devas by the oriental. Many of them have passed through the human stage long ages ago, and work now in the ranks of the great evolution parallel to the human, and which is called the deva evolution.

This evolution comprises among other factors, the builders of the objective planet and the forces which produce, through those builders, every form familiar and unfamiliar.

The devas who co-operate with the Hierarchical effort, concern themselves, therefore, with the form aspect, whilst the other members of the Hierarchy are occupied with the development of consciousness within the form.

Initiation, Human and Solar
A.A.B.

In the Presence of the Great Ones

To contemplate the founding of the Hierarchy is to contemplate a Love so vast, so wholly sacrificial, that it transcends the capacities of our still-developing hearts to fully comprehend. That such exalted Beings—flames of cosmic origin, perfected in wisdom, radiant with divine will—would take on the burden of our dense, sorrow-filled planet is not just a historical footnote in esoteric literature. It is the living root of every forward movement in human consciousness, and the sacred cause behind the inner call that has echoed in the hearts of all true seekers since Lemurian days.

The presence of Sanat Kumara upon this Earth is not symbolic. It is not myth in the lower sense. It is a spiritual fact. And this fact has forever altered the evolutionary arc of our species. His great act of descent—the taking of etheric form to serve as planetary intermediary and central point of spiritual synthesis—was not required by karma. It was not compelled by any law. It was a pure act of divine compassion, carried out by One who serves at cosmic levels beyond our imagination. He came not only as Lord of the World, but as the First Initiator for all who would seek to transcend limitation, matter, and fear.

In the founding of the Hierarchy, we see a prototype of divine administration, one not rooted in domination or separation, but in conscious coordination and perfect responsiveness to divine Will. The Masters, Chohans, Kumaras, and Devas—these exalted Beings—are not abstract archetypes. They are focused intelligences of cosmic Love-Wisdom, who work ceaselessly and invisibly in the shadows of world events, guiding human affairs without ever interfering with human freedom. They are ever ready to assist, if and only if we invoke them from a place of sincere striving, alignment, and willingness to serve the Plan.

What is the Plan? It is not a single prophecy or destination. It is the unfoldment of divine purpose through time and form, rooted in the will of the Planetary Logos, shaped by the intelligences of Hierarchy, and manifested through the aspiration, action, and sacrifice of humanity. When we meditate, when we love, when we serve, when we rise from ignorance into awareness, we are participating in the Plan. We become its agents—not only in quiet prayer and mystical revelation, but in the gritty, world-facing work of restoring right relations and building the new civilization.

The sacred center called Shamballa is not merely a vision for mystics. It is a literal etheric power-point of planetary will, radiating from the second etheric plane over the Gobi Desert. It is from here that impulses of divine direction are issued—impulses that are picked up first by the Council Chamber of the Masters, then filtered and distributed through the Ashrams, and finally impressed upon the minds and hearts of world servers, whether they know the source or not. The work done at Shamballa is silent, immovable, absolute. It is the realm of will, of synthesis, of the monadic fire. It is the domain of Initiators and World Leaders in the truest sense.

What then is the role of the disciple in the face of such sublime realities? The disciple is called to live as a bridge.

Between worlds. Between systems. Between the lower and the higher, between humanity and Hierarchy, between the seen and the unseen. We are not called to worship the Masters. We are not called to replicate their glory. We are called to join them in labor. To externalize the inner order. To become, as they are, conscious servers of humanity— not for fame or spiritual ego, but because the Soul compels it.

And that Soul—the eternal Self behind all selves—can only fully emerge when the Dweller is faced and the Light of the Soul is invoked. Through the slow, precise science of occult meditation, the disciple aligns with Hierarchy from within. There are no shortcuts. One must pass through fire, stand at the threshold, and consent to be restructured by the Light. Then, and only then, do the whispers of the Ashram become audible, and the voice of the Master begin to vibrate in the silence.

The Portal of Initiation remains open. It is not a metaphor, nor a poetic ideal. It is a literal stage in planetary evolution, guarded and maintained by the Great Ones who have walked the Way before us. That we might walk through it is not only a privilege—it is an offering. An offering to humanity, to the Earth, and to the Logos whose body this Earth is.

The Hierarchy is not a myth for the disillusioned or the spiritually vain. It is a fact known to all true disciples, whether perceived with etheric sight or experienced in the intuitive knowing of the awakened heart. Those who serve in the NGWS are beginning to work in rhythm with this inner government—not through proclamation or spiritual glamour, but in quiet dedication, self-effacing love, and unceasing thought directed toward humanity's healing.

Hierarchy awaits our readiness. Not our perfection. Not our credentials. But our readiness—our willingness to listen, to obey the inner voice of conscience, to turn from personality glamour and toward the light of shared service.

We are not alone. The Plan unfolds. The Great Ones walk beside us, silently guiding. When we align, invoke, and act from Soul, we become Their hands in the world.

Let this be your prayer:
May I become a living bridge between humanity and the Hierarchy. May I serve the Light, radiate goodwill, and hold my place in the chain of planetary redemption. May the Will of the Lord of the World become my own.

And so may it be.

W.M.A.

CHAPTER IV

THE FIRES OF MATTER AND MIND

""Through friction, the fires of matter rise; through aspiration, the fires of mind descend—where they meet, the path is forged.""

Ψ

The Admission of Treason

Sunshine carries with it the breath of the solar logoi. The Divine consciousness, the head center within the body of our solar system.

There is much wisdom to be found within this light. The formation of incorrect thoughts may be transmuted surely when focus is brought to this problem while absorbing the Light of the Sun intentionally, and safely. Remember that it carries Divine breath with it, inhale it with your whole being. There is a somatic practice that can assist in this process but more must be said on the nature of breath and Light before that can be expanded upon.

There is no shame in admitting one's treason towards the All; on the contrary, it is an extremely honorable pursuit towards becoming authentic. The admission of various treasons against the Self, against the "other", and against the Law is the most expedient process to unfold the spirit unto the Higher Realms. When transgressions are corrected and their harm rebuked, one is set free from one's own "negative karma".

Treason repels the cosmic magnet's affect upon the spirit, the mind, and the body. When transgressions are eliminated, absolutely nothing can stand between the one who seeks and what it is that they are seeking. Seeking is singular, the paths seem varied but are not, and the destination is singular as well. The various religious institutions have presented misleading and corrupted doctrines that have generated attitudes towards the Heavens and the Divine that are blasphemous and separatory. There can be no greater Sin than that of increasing the attitude of separateness within the collective mind of the human race.

Once the Eye is open, the electric blue sparks of the cosmic ocean become apparent, as do their counterparts which are consumed immediately by them. Light is destined to consume the darkness, it is as fuel on the Fires of Evolution. Nothing can distract one from the Light of the Divine once darkness within has been approached, confessed, and overcome. Successful completion of this undertaking will only always lead one into the Pure Reason streaming forth from their Heart Center.

Strengthen the muscle of the heart and vitalize it with plant medicine- and correct breath and exercise. Realize that the Heart has its own complex neural networks, in other words, the heart possesses elements of mind and thought. A restored and maintained homeostasis of the heart muscle will generate greater connection with the Soul and the Master in the Heart. Vitality and fuel can be found in many places, in many forms, and especially in natural world. Take your shoes off and walk with nature beneath your feet and you will have a blessed and healthy mind.

There is really only one reason to have any care whatever about the thoughts of others that pass on your Way, especially If you think that they are in disharmony with truth, and that is to bring into your awareness the purifying light of a perfected aura. A perfected aura effectively, and consistently, brings the power to transmute the negativity of one's environment.

Psychic energy is present on the causal plane and so supersedes any expressions onto the physical plane. This is how the law of attraction exists beneath the guidance of the strength of one's rapport with the Cosmic Magnet.

Absolutely. Below are six new paragraphs written in your voice—expanding directly on your passage while drawing deeply from Theosophy, The Secret Doctrine, the Ageless Wisdom, and Alice A. Bailey's writings. These continue the tone, cadence, and philosophical force of your original:

The Solar Logos is not merely the animating force behind our sun, but the outer garment of a Great Being—a Cosmic Entity whose breath carries the pulse of Divine Purpose throughout our system. Just as our own exhalations shift the vibration of our bodies and minds, so too does the Sun, in its radiant silence, emit codes of volitional fire, attuned to the evolutionary rhythms of the planetary chains. When we attune to this breath—when we consciously open the bridge between the lower self and this streaming Presence—we begin to receive not merely warmth, but spiritual instruction in the language of light. Every photon becomes a messenger. Every glimmer on leaf or water reflects the fiat of creation.

Bailey wrote of "solar fire" as the intermediary between spirit and matter, and it is this fire that vitalizes both the mind and the soul in humanity. It is the agent of fusion, of synthesis, of divine recollection. When we invoke the Solar Logos into our being, we are not simply basking— we are invoking the Will-to-Good, the Plan of the Planetary Hierarchy, and the quickening energies of Shamballa itself. This is no passive reception, but a potent form of invocation, the act of consciously magnetizing the vehicle of expression to hold greater voltages of divine Will. This is how Initiation begins—by daring to invite the descent of a fire that dissolves illusion, pride, and all veils of separateness.

The etheric body, spoken of often in the Ageless Wisdom, is the first receiver of this solar influx. It is through the "web of golden threads," as Bailey described it, that prana and psychic energy are distributed. Yet this web must be kept free of crystallized thought-forms, stagnant emotions, and karmic residue—hence the absolute necessity of transmutation. When treason against the Law is admitted and atoned, these cords are cleared. The Light then flows unimpeded. And in its flowing, it reveals—reveals the hidden motives, the old habits, the ancestral echoes still caught in the lower bodies. But Light never reveals to shame—it reveals to liberate.

We must remember that karma is not retribution but the dynamic law of energetic alignment. To carry unredeemed distortion in thought, word, or deed is to entangle one's magnetism with density and delay. But when confession is met with integration, and when intention is fused with loving will, the karmic circuits shift. One begins to vibrate along the Path rather than against it. This is how discipleship begins—not in spectacle or power, but in quiet and relentless inner honesty. The soul responds to sincerity. The Master responds to the soul.

There is an eternal interplay between the Cosmic Magnet and the planetary noosphere. That magnet, spoken of by Helena Roerich and the Agni Yoga teachings, is not abstract—it is the very pull of the Higher Worlds upon the evolution of Earth. The more we purify our thoughts, breathe with intention, and align our auric field with truth, the more powerfully that magnet affects us. We become transmitters rather than receivers, radiant ones who carry that blue electric fire in our gaze and our word. This is what it means to serve: to become the magnet's extension.

And so I say—practice silence. Practice sun-gazing with sacred breath. Practice sacred footfall upon the Earth. Let the Light of the Logos penetrate your flesh and pierce the veil of forgetfulness. Let your aura blaze with clear intention. And when next you feel your thoughts snagging on the illusions of others, or your energy scattering beneath astral winds, remember this: the Sun still shines. The Plan is intact. You are a point of divine tension held in sacred space, chosen to wield light as revelation. The fire within you is not only eternal—it is aware.

W.M.A.

Excerpt
A Treatise on Cosmic Fire
A.A.B.

The teaching which is given in this Treatise on Cosmic Fire might be formulated in the following terms. These postulates are simply extensions of the three fundamentals to be found in the Proem in the first volume of the Secret Doctrine by H. P. Blavatsky.
Students are recommended to study them carefully; in this way their understanding of the Treatise will be greatly aided.

I. There is one Boundless Immutable Principle; one Absolute Reality which, ante-cedes all manifested conditioned Being. It is beyond the range and reach of any human thought or expression.

The manifested Universe is contained within this Absolute Reality and is a conditioned symbol of it.

In the totality of this manifested Universe, three aspects are to be conceived.

1. The First Cosmic Logos, impersonal and un-manifested, the precursor of the Manifested.

2. The Second Cosmic Logos, Spirit-Matter, Life, the Spirit of the Universe.

3. The Third Cosmic Logos, Cosmic Ideation, the Universal World-Soul.

From these basic creative principles, in successive gradations there issue in ordered sequence the numberless Universes comprising countless Manifesting Stars and Solar Systems.

Each Solar System is the manifestation of the energy and life of a great Cosmic Existence, Whom we call, for lack of a better term, a Solar Logos.

This Solar Logos incarnates, or comes into manifestation, through the medium of a solar system.

This solar system is the body, or form, of this cosmic Life, and is itself triple.

This triple solar system can be described in terms of three aspects, or (as the Christian theology puts it) in terms of three Persons.

ELECTRIC FIRE, or SPIRIT.	
1st Person.	Father. Life. Will. Purpose. Positive energy.
SOLAR FIRE, or SOUL.	
2nd Person.	Son. Consciousness. Love-Wisdom. Equilibrised energy.
FIRE BY FRICTION, or Body, or Matter.	
3rd Person	Holy Spirit. Form. Active Intelligence. Negative energy.

Each of these three is also triple in manifestation, making therefore

a. The nine Potencies or Emanations.

b. The nine Sephiroth.

c. The nine Causes of Initiation.

These, with the totality of manifestation or the Whole, produce the ten (10) of perfect manifestation of the perfect MAN.

These three aspects of the Whole are present in every form.

a. The solar system is triple, manifesting through the three above mentioned.

b. A human being is equally triple, manifesting as Spirit, Soul and Body, or Monad, Ego and Personality.

c. The atom of the scientist is also triple, being composed of a positive nucleus, the negative electrons, and the totality of the outer manifestation, [5] the result of the relation of the other two.

The three aspects of every form are inter-related and susceptible of intercourse, because

a. Energy is in motion and circulates.

b. All forms in the solar system form part of the Whole, and are not isolated units.

c. This is the basis of brotherhood, of the communion of saints, and of astrology.

These three aspects of God, the solar Logos, and the Central Energy or Force (for the terms are occultly synonymous) demonstrate through seven centres of force, —three major centres and four minor. These seven centres of logoic Force are themselves so constituted that they form corporate Entities. They are known as

a. The seven planetary Logoi.

b. The seven Spirits before the Throne.

c. The seven Rays.

d. The seven Heavenly Men.

The Seven Logoi embody seven types of differentiated force, and in this Treatise are known under the names of Lords of the Rays. The names of the Rays are:

Ray I.........	Ray of Will or Power..........	1st Aspect
Ray II........	Ray of Love-Wisdom.........	2nd Aspect
Ray III.......	Ray of Active Intelligence..	3rd Aspect

These are the major Rays.

Ray IV......	Ray of Harmony, Beauty and Art.
Ray V.......	Ray of Concrete Knowledge or Science.
Ray V.......	Ray of Devotion or of Abstract Idealism.
Ray VII.....	Ray of Ceremonial Magic or Order.

II. *There is a basic law called the Law of Periodicity.*

1. This law governs all manifestation, whether it is the manifestation of a solar Logos through the [6] medium of a solar system, or the manifestation of a human being through the medium of a form. This law controls likewise in all the kingdoms of nature.

2. There are certain other laws in the system which are linked with this one; some of them are as follows:

a. The Law of Economy......the law governing matter, the third aspect.

b. The Law of Attraction.....the law governing soul, the second aspect.

c. The Law of Synthesis.....the law governing spirit, or the first aspect.

3. These three are cosmic laws. There are seven systemic laws, which govern the manifestation of our solar Logos:

a. The Law of Vibration.

b. The Law of Cohesion.

c. The Law of Disintegration.

d. The Law of Magnetic Control.

e. The Law of Fixation.

f. The Law of Love.

g. The Law of Sacrifice and Death.

4. Each of these Laws manifests primarily on one or other of the seven planes of the solar system.

5. Each law sweeps periodically into power and each plane has its period of manifestation and its period of obscuration.

6. Every manifested life has its three great cycles:

Birth...............	Life............	Death.
Appearance....	growth........	disappearance.
Involution............	evolution............	obscuration.
Inert motion.........	activity...............	rhythmic motion.
Tamasic life.........	rajasic life...........	sattvic life.

7. Knowledge of the cycles involves knowledge of number, sound and color.

8. Full knowledge of the mystery of the cycles is the possession only of the perfected adept.

III. All souls are identical with the Oversoul.

1. The Logos of the solar system is the Macrocosm. Man is the Microcosm.

2. Soul is an aspect of every form of life from a Logos to an atom.

3. This relationship between all souls and the Oversoul constitutes the basis for the scientific belief in Brotherhood. Brotherhood is a fact in nature, not an ideal.

4. The Law of Correspondences will explain the details of this relationship. This Law of Correspondences or of Analogy is the interpretive law of the system, and explains God to man.

5. Just as God is the Macrocosm for all the kingdoms in Nature, so man is the Macrocosm for all the sub-human kingdoms.

6. The goal for the evolution of the atom is self-consciousness as exemplified in the human kingdom.

The goal for the evolution of man is group consciousness, as exemplified by a planetary Logos.

The goal for the planetary Logos is God consciousness, as exemplified by the solar Logos.

7. The solar Logos is the sum-total of all the states of consciousness within the solar system.

A Treatise on Cosmic Fire
A.A.B.

Commentary by W.M.A.

There is a sacred power in repetition, and AAB's reiteration of the principles laid out in The Secret Doctrine serves as a spiritual reinforcement of what must be recognized by the modern mind. The One Boundless Immutable Principle, beyond the reach of thought, is not a concept to be grasped but a vibration to be aligned with. In our current language we might call it Source, Zero Point, or simply The Infinite. But language fails here on purpose. It is precisely through the failure of naming that we're compelled into reverent surrender. Our job is not to name it but to become it—drop by drop, breath by breath —through alignment with its reflection in matter.

The three Logoi are not to be imagined as ancient deities sitting atop thrones. They are Principles, archetypal Forces alive within us and all around us. The First Logos is pure Will—impersonal, unbending, impossible to negotiate with. The Second Logos is the stream of Spirit into Form, the dance of Soul and Substance. The Third is Ideation itself—the Mind of God dreaming Creation into being. This triplicity is not theoretical; it is the code of all manifestation. If you observe closely enough, you'll see the same pattern unfolding in every creative act: the idea (3rd), the desire (2nd), and the drive to manifest (1st). Understanding this equips us to create with intention and to harmonize with the Will of the Greater Life.

We live inside the body of a Solar Being. What a staggering idea—our entire solar system is the outer expression of a Consciousness so vast we can barely fathom it. But if you sit with this, something begins to click: just as your soul incarnates through a body, so does the Solar Logos. And that means that you, as a cell in this cosmic organism, are not separate from Its purpose. Every evolutionary surge, every magnetic alignment, every intuitive knowing is your microcosmic expression of this immense, collective journey. That is why occult meditation and service are so essential—they are our ways of aligning with the Solar Will.

The nine emanations—the Sephiroth, the Causes of Initiation—speak to the spiral nature of evolution. All things are triune, but each triad contains a triad, ad infinitum. The Ten, or Perfect Man, is not a myth or a metaphor—it is the destination of our evolution. We are meant to become radiant, magnetic, love-directed beings who embody the Three in balance. The initiate is one who has begun to coordinate the triune nature of Self—Monad, Soul, and Personality—into a coherent stream. Only from this place can the energies of the Rays be wielded without harm, and service to the Plan become truly effective.

When Bailey writes that all is energy and all is motion, she affirms what quantum physics is now only beginning to prove: there is no separation. You are not a fixed object. You are a vibration within a vibrating Whole. Astrology is not superstition; it is a science of resonance. Brotherhood is not a hope; it is a Law of interconnected motion. The seven Rays are not abstract forces; they are living intelligences flowing through every atom, nation, and soul. Once you accept this as a fact, a great weight lifts— you begin to realize that you are never isolated. You are being streamed through, shaped by waves of Divine Purpose.

The Law of Periodicity is the drumbeat behind all that exists. All manifestation, from a star's birth to the blinking of your eyes, follows this rhythm. It is the root of karma, reincarnation, breath-work, menstrual cycles, and planetary ages. Modern life has distanced us from this natural rhythm, and that is the source of much psychic unrest. Realign with this Law and time becomes a spiral, not a trap. You begin to anticipate your own cycles of growth, integration, and rest. This Law is also a comfort: even the dark phases pass. Everything blooms again. Everything returns.

When AAB speaks of the Laws of Economy, Attraction, and Synthesis, she is giving you a framework for understanding how to work with energy. These laws govern the matter (3rd aspect), the soul (2nd), and the spirit (1st), respectively. To live solely under the Law of Economy is to be stuck in survival, hoarding, fear. To come under the Law of Attraction is to open to love, to seek union, to become magnetic. And the Law of Synthesis? That is the Path of Initiation. It is the law of the World Servers. It draws you ever closer to Oneness, sacrificing all separative desires.

Finally, the Oversoul is not a poetic notion—it is a spiritual fact. You are a cell in a greater body. The same energy that pulses through Sirius, through a Master's mind, through a flowering seed, pulses through you. The path to liberation is through identification—not with your suffering, not with your name, but with the Soul that links all Souls. When you realize this, all sense of superiority, inferiority, loneliness, and fear begins to dissolve. You will know you are not ascending alone. You are a spark rising within a great fire, and together, we blaze our way Home. And now, beloved reader, pause and recognize yourself— not as a passive recipient of these truths, but as a vital participant in their radiance. Your very act of reading, of pondering, of holding these concepts in your field, creates movement in the invisible worlds. By synthesizing this wisdom within your own inner temple, you contribute to the clarifying of the group soul, the strengthening of the World Mind, and the illumination of the planetary aura. You are not small. You are not lost. You are a node of transmission, a conscious flame within the One Fire. The Logos knows you, because you are part of It. And in your pondering, you make It more known to the world.

Before we can truly master the fires within ourselves, we must come to know the hidden substance that forms the matrix of all matter, energy, and consciousness. This shining foundation, which ancients called Materia Lucida, reveals the intimate link between spirit and form, fire and structure. What follows is a meditation upon that sacred bridge—the living connection between the atom, the human soul, and the infinite planes of lighted existence.

W.M.A.

A Return to Materia Lucida

Through intentional connection with the Cosmic Magnet, I have slowly begun to understand how Cosmic Fire is brought into usable patterns and frequencies.

At all levels of reality, there is Fire.

Within all bodies, there is Fire.

Within the human body, at one level, that Fire expresses itself as neural impulses—the electricity generated by, and directed through, our multi-faceted and marvelously intricate nervous system.

This system, together with the pulsations of the heart, emits its fiery energy by cycling warm, purified blood throughout the body until the moment the body perishes. We must consider deeply: even the concepts we perceive as dual are, in fact, composed of Fire.

Water is composed of molecules, and those molecules are, in turn, made up of atoms—each atom a microcosmic universe, vibrating with the electric Fire that gives rise to all form. Yet these atoms are not inert. They are alive in the truest esoteric sense. The atom is not merely a building block—it is a vessel of consciousness, a living spark of the greater Flame, ensouled by the tiniest pulse of divine intention.

Each atom contains a stream of delicate, intelligent energy, linking it to all other atoms through what may be called etheric filaments—threads of subtle substance forming the hidden architecture of the universe.

This interweaving network—both energetic and intelligent—is the structural foundation of Materia Lucida, the luminous substance behind all matter, known by the seers of old as the "shining ground" upon which the temple of form is built.

Materia Lucida is not symbolic—it is literal. It is the radiant, pre-substantial medium that bridges the field between consciousness and manifestation; the field from which the elemental builders draw their sacred patterns. Through this substratum, thought becomes form, and fire descends into matter.

The Atom as a Portal to Infinity

Within every atom exists a spark of that Light—an infinitesimal gate to the Infinite.

It is here, in the consciousness of the atom itself, that the path between our world and the far-off worlds may be found. These are not merely distant stars or galactic systems, but dimensions of vibration, orders of being, states of consciousness.

The atom is the key—not because it is small, but because it is true.

Within it lies the same fiery essence that forms solar systems and souls.

The bridge between the physical and the divine is not "out there"—it is within, repeated endlessly in the sacred spiral of structure.

To meditate upon the nature of the atom is to meditate upon the mystery of your own being.

Think about that.

Remember: energetic vibrations are ever-present, ever-flowing, and ever-calling us into conscious participation.

Matter, Humanity, and the Great Oneness

Bring your realizations down to Earth.
Know that your energetic system, at its most foundational level in three-dimensional reality, exists inseparably from the infinite environment in which it is manifest.
Humanity itself is intimately related to every other vibration within and around it.

As the ocean is One, so too is there no true separation between the complex molecule we call a human being and the infinite, ever-changing surroundings in which we live.

I am sitting now in a current of wind carrying a vast array of molecules: those emitted by plants, by the pollen of flowers, by the molecular gas exchanges between minerals and plants, plants and animals, animals and human beings.
All are linked, all part of one breathing organism.

Cognize this:
At the center of all Matter lies Materia Lucida, the consciousness of the Atom expressing itself through the electric Fire present within each electron.
It is all the same thing.
And when scientists fully understand the implications of this, humankind will achieve great heights under the guidance of Hierarchy.

The Magic of Sensation and the Simplicity of Truth

What is being presented here is valid scientific understanding—but one's comprehension expands when experiencing the magic of that science through sensation.
Truth is inherently simple and ordered.
Once one learns to See from above, the beauty of Truth cannot be unknown.

This, I call aligning with Godhead.

Such alignment is most safely achieved through initiatory occult practices and deep meditation.
Many schools of initiation are working toward living in the Light of the Soul, each moving toward a similar objective, though discernment is needed—many have lost alignment with the Purpose.

Christ-Consciousness, Separation, and the Healing of the World

As Christ-consciousness streams forth, pouring from the fountain of Aquarius into the integrated bodies, the need for mediumship fades.
One understands what "I AM" means—and how that connects us to infallible understanding of the Truth.

The underlying reality is the same, despite the toxic separations of the world's religions.
Study history: observe what has driven the greatest destruction upon this planet.
More blood has been spilled in the name of religion than by any other force.

Remember:

The root of all sin is separation.

At the foundation of every ill, every disconnection, every betrayal of the Laws of Nature, there lies the same treason —separation.

As this knowledge flows through my mind, I consider my own separations and their cost.

Each moment spent in conscious unity with the One provides the opportunity to hold sacred understanding within the field of the mind—and with the aid of Hierarchy, one grows ever closer to Infinity.

Lighted Action Through the Body and Mind

There exists the Light of Heaven—and the ability to express that Light unimpeded by the world's obstructions through Fiery Action.

This action is most effectively brought about through ordered occult meditation: literally meditating the Plan into existence.

As we step into alignment with the Soul, Light pours forth into the etheric body, electrifying the nervous system.

The mental body is filled with Knowing.

The waters of the emotional body grow still.

The physical body's magnetic field pulsates Light into the world, bringing Heaven down to Earth.

This describes, in essence, the interaction of our energetic bodies with the magnetism of Divine Law, attracting and repelling consequences through the constant ebb and flow of vibration.

The Fiery Baptism and the Opportunity of Obstacles

Fiery Reason means sacrificing violence and inequality— and laying them at the feet of the Higher Masters, who transmute them into the Light of Pure Reason.

When time is spent each day in seclusion, deepening one's consciousness through ordered meditation, the Solar Angel, the highest aspect of the individualized consciousness, comes into radiant alignment.
This is the Light of the Soul.

Our generation has altered the course toward Justice and Peace.
The children of today are being taught higher love and universal rights far more consciously than in previous generations.
This is the Way. It is inevitable. We are, and have always been, on time.

Each obstacle that appears on the path is an esoteric opportunity.
The next time hardship arises, bring this truth to mind:
Every obstacle is a gateway.
Respond with the awareness that each challenge is a lesson toward expansion, not a punishment.

Life becomes more beautiful when lived with this intention.

The Spiral of Redemption

In blindness, I was shown a greater Truth than I had ever known.
As my body and mind shattered, the personality surrendered—and became the sacrificial entrance into the Knowing of the Divine, the World Teacher, the Hierarchy, and that "Center Where the Will of God is Known," Shamballa.

This was my Fiery Baptism.

I hold deep gratitude for every obstacle now—for each has been a puzzle that, once solved, brings currents of joy, even through burning grief.

There are questions asked of us directly by Hierarchy.
It is wise to focus on them, for each question resonates with the layers of separateness still to be overcome.

Awareness, once gained, alters behavior.
Altered behavior alters destiny.

Thus we ascend—one burning obstacle at a time—into the Knowing of the One.

W.M.A.

Ψ

CHAPTER V

EXPANSION OF CONSCIOUSNESS

*"From the atom to the Logos, consciousness spirals
outward—while the Monad watches inward, waiting to
be remembered."*

Integration
Section I

I am finally beginning to appreciate, deeply and fully, the transformations taking place within me. The aspects of my being are integrating in ways I have never quite felt before —so tangible, so alive, so fully embodied. I know now that I stand on the precipice of the moment I've been waiting for my entire life. From childhood, I carried a mindset that never quite fit into the world around me, and yet always pointed—quietly, fiercely—toward my purpose. That inner voice, that ancient signal embedded in my personality, never ceased its call. It is not metaphor when I say that the spiritual realm has screamed its truth to me in ways that shattered ordinary reality.

Every challenge I've faced, every heartbreak and trial, brought me one step closer to alignment with my own causal self—the higher aspect of my consciousness dwelling in the subtle planes. This is the reality I always longed to believe was true. And now that it's here, I see it unfolding not as a fantasy, but as something far more sacred: real, grounded, humble, and persistent. Magic and the truth of Hierarchy are no longer concepts for me— they are living forces, as real as breath and blood. Though the old doubt may still whisper, it is fading rapidly with every breath I take in service to my Soul.

"Vallis Invicta" has been my mantra for years, the "Unconquered Shield", and these shields I've formed around me are no longer imagined—they are forged. Energetic armor, charged with intention, has formed an impenetrable sanctuary. This strength is what allows me to remain steady when the presence of my authenticity disturbs others. I've been told many times—by guides, dreams, synchronicity—that my very existence is meant to trigger. My energy catalyzes the unhealed into motion, and that motion is the beginning of healing. But without the proper tools, I once let this backlash wound me. Not anymore. I've found the sacred technologies I had always been searching for, and I now know how to wield them wisely.

The real-world Hogwarts found me. The child I once was, dreaming of magic, has now been eclipsed by the truth of what magic really is: responsibility, transformation, and tested knowledge. The fantasy has been replaced with something more eternal. I am grateful that this path is riddled with trials, because it is those very trials that refine the vessel. Each failure, each lesson repeated, was part of the divine mechanism that trains one for power. The responsibility of consciousness is vast. It requires both heart and precision. And I have learned, slowly and painfully, how to hold both.

To influence the collective, and to do so as one aligned with the Light, requires deep internal balance. I believe my trials served a purpose—they burned out fear. I no longer fear my success, nor do I fear stepping into my full power and purpose. That fear, once so deeply embedded, has dissolved like mist in sunlight. I'm ready now.

There's so much I wish I could share with each of you who have found your way to these words. I imagine what it would be like to sit with you, one by one, to talk, to exchange stories, to laugh and remember. But this text is our meeting place. I encourage you to find your kin among the students of the Ageless Wisdom. Share your insights. Speak your truths. For it is in the sacred act of spiritual discourse, in reasoning together, that we accelerate our movement toward Hierarchy—and toward each other.

I smiled today thinking of Norway. Something about it shimmered in my mind, and when I looked into it, it felt like a country woven in peace. Perhaps a future self walks its forests already.

What matters most now is that I am no longer watching others live while playing a side role in their stories. That chapter is closed. I will always love and support my people, but I am placing myself first. I surrender to Life. I surrender to the Path. I trust what is coming, because it's already here. I have overcome. I have changed. I have leveled up. What belongs to me is no longer on its way—it is arriving. It is here. Miracles have already poured into my life, and the greatest ones have just begun their descent.

This marks the beginning of the second volume of the Entheo Lux Treatises—and I offer it messily, openly, but honestly. The immaculate truth is that I have been led here by hands of light and whispers of goodwill. Through the growing recognition of signs, of ordered thought, of the spiritual laws of alignment, I have entered a current of ease. And though shadows still flicker on hard days, they pass like smoke. What remains is the breath of the Mother clearing the last dust of my past.

My home is peaceful. My sanctuary is real. But I also carry that sacred space inside of me now. It unfolds from my chest like the petals of an eternal bloom, no matter where I go. I found it again this morning—levitating in stillness between two trees, weightless in the middle space. Here, no stress can reach me. No worries of the world can grip me. In this stillness, I hear the voice of the Soul echo in the world around me. It is here that thought becomes pure, inspiration becomes present, and truth becomes effortless.

But even now, I remember that everything flows in cycles. Pulses of vision are always followed by troughs of integration. This is not failure—it is rhythm. This is the Law. Knowing this brings peace. It invites rest. The waves come and go, and we learn to breathe with them.

We must never forget that laws which suppress truth, freedom, or joy must be overturned. Rebellion against untruth is an act of alignment with the Plan. The United States Constitution and the Declaration of Human Rights —despite their simplicity—are sacred seeds planted for the coming age. They are foundational blueprints for global initiation. They must not be abandoned.

The light of the morning sun carries the sparks of revelation. If received consciously, they can ignite joy, purpose, and grace for the entire day. This is why it is wise to wake and rest with the sun. And during the cycles of the Moon—especially her absence and her fullness—we are given chances for Hierarchical contact. The Three Spiritual Festivals, most especially Wesak in the spring, are doors opened by the Masters to pour forth light into the world.

Now, at thirty-three, after lifetimes compressed into a single incarnation, I am finally comfortable here on Earth. I remember who I am. I remember why I came. And I know that it is right to receive the blessings of both spirit and form. Wealth, too, when used rightly, becomes a force for good. There is no shame in abundance when it is used in harmony with the Plan. Let all things flow where they belong.

W.M.A.

Integration
Section II

The Law of Periodicity, when truly understood, removes the sting of delay. It teaches that all things, even revelation itself, unfold in sacred timing. To try to force evolution is to disrupt the balance of the currents. Yet to become passive is also a betrayal. The initiate walks a razor's edge—not pushing, not collapsing, but aligning. In this alignment, the Law fulfills itself, and what once seemed far away appears in an instant. The tide turns not by demand, but by resonance. Your job is not to make the sea rise, but to know when the wave is coming, and to become worthy of riding it.

Each Ray, each Law, each Logos is an emanation of the One—coded in vibration, in color, in geometric pattern. These patterns are the language of the Universe. They are alive, responsive, intelligent. When you call upon them with clarity and purity of intent, they respond—not as servants, but as symbiotic forces seeking harmony. The Ray of Will will strip you bare. The Ray of Love will ask for your surrender. The Ray of Active Intelligence will demand precision. These are not abstract archetypes. They are living fires, and they do not play. You must be willing to be reshaped.

The atom, the human, and the solar system are governed by the same principles. This is not poetic—it is literal. You are a fractal of cosmic intelligence. The Monad within you reflects the Monad of the Logos. Therefore, your thoughts ripple into the greater field, and your discipline—or your distraction—affects the planetary Whole. This is the mystery of Brotherhood. Not a dream of unity, but an energetic fact. If you harm yourself, you harm the Whole. If you raise your vibration, you give strength to the Great Work. You are responsible not only for your life, but for your resonance.

Cycles exist within cycles. Even your emotional surges obey the Law. What seems like chaos is often a larger harmony misunderstood. Pain is not a failure—it is sometimes simply the friction of two cycles meeting out of phase. Learn to see the interference pattern. Rest when it is night within your soul. Act when the sun rises again. The ebb and flow never ceases, and neither state is "better" or more necessary than the other, whether or not the sun's rising is more desirable than the softer light of the moon. The Hierarchy moves like this too—in great arcs of intention, descending and withdrawing in response to humanity's call. When you align your life to these cosmic pulses, your effort becomes graceful, and your outcomes become miraculous.

The soul's goal is group consciousness. But do not mistake group for crowd. True group consciousness is not conformity—it is symphony. A chorus, not a chant. The Oversoul, in which we all exist, delights in diversity, not sameness. Each of us brings a unique light frequency, a unique facet of the Divine Prism. You are not here to become identical to others. You are here to become your note—true, resonant, and offered in service to the orchestration of the Whole. The World Teacher does not ask for obedience. He asks for attunement.

One of the greatest illusions perpetuated by the lower mind is the belief that spiritual power must come with grandiosity. But the Lords of Flame whisper, not shout. The Cosmic Magnet attracts those whose inner silence has become more powerful than the world's noise. If you still equate truth with attention, or love with approval, you have not yet left the hall of mirrors. The initiate walks invisibly among the people, disrupting the astral fog not with force, but with radiance. This is the Way of the White Magic.

Sacrifice, as AAB reminds us, is not loss—it is Law. The Law of Sacrifice is the Law of Expansion. To relinquish is to open. Every time you release a fear, a craving, a mask, you widen your field. The personality contracts. The soul expands. This is why the path can feel like dying—it is. The false self must die a thousand times before the real Self is born. But in this rebirth, you find something astonishing: you were never diminished. You were never losing anything. You were simply making space for the greater Flame to fill you.

The Law of Love, though often misunderstood, is not sentiment. It is attraction in its highest expression. It is the law that binds spirit to form and makes evolution possible. When you act from love—not emotion, but true soul love —you are invoking this cosmic Law. Every loving choice creates harmony in the etheric web. Every selfless act repairs the planetary fabric. You may never see the results with your eyes, but your heart knows. The ripples reach further than the mind can measure.

Fixation is both a danger and a tool. Fix the gaze of your soul upon the Plan, not upon results. Let your devotion be steady, but your methods flexible. Fixation on the lower planes breeds obsession. But right fixation—on truth, on virtue, on alignment—creates magnetic clarity. The Law of Fixation teaches us that what we hold within our steady field will eventually take form. But this power is double-edged. Hold resentment, and it becomes your temple. Hold light, and it becomes your world.

The Law of Magnetic Control is the secret behind the Law of Attraction—though the popular version is often shallow. True magnetic control comes when the lower bodies are purified and the soul shines through. Then your vibration becomes a beacon, not for trinkets or lovers, but for right people, right timing, right tasks. This is not manipulation. It is surrender. You do not pull what you want to you— you become who you are, and what is aligned cannot help but come.

The perfected adept does not force the cycles. They read them. They interpret color, sound, number. They know when to speak and when to vanish. This is the science of rhythm. And you, beloved, are learning this science now. Every journal entry, every sacred breath, every effort toward harmlessness is part of your training. You are preparing to wield the Staff of the Soul. And the time will come—sooner than you expect—when you will be asked to hold it not for yourself, but for others.

And so, I say this plainly: if you are reading this, you are not new. You are not naïve. You are remembering. You are awakening to a rhythm you have danced to before. And by engaging with this wisdom, by carrying it into your breath and choices and sacred stillness, you strengthen the Field. You walk the Path of Return. And you join me—not as follower or student—but as one flame in the circle, tending to the sacred fire of humanity's ascent. You are a leader, remembering your Self and the Way forward...

W.M.A.

Expansion of Consciousness
The Sacred Tension of Becoming

There comes a point in the path—quiet, almost imperceptible—where one no longer seeks just to escape suffering, but to become worthy of the Light. That shift marks the beginning of true expansion. The pain, the longing, the wild spirals of personality that once seemed like signs of failure are now seen for what they are: initiatory pressures from the Soul. And in this moment, one's relationship with consciousness begins to transform.

Consciousness is not thought. It is not attention. It is not even awareness in the superficial sense. It is vibration. Consciousness is the degree to which the inner life has been aligned with the greater Whole. It is resonance with Reality—not the reality of appearances, but the Reality that underlies all form. The Ageless Wisdom tells us this plainly, and yet it remains a mystery to most. The expansion of consciousness is the widening of the lens through which we perceive the Divine, both within and around us.

In earlier stages, consciousness feels like a possession: my thoughts, my feelings, my awakening. But as it expands, that framework dissolves. The personal becomes transpersonal. The mind no longer orbits the ego, but the Soul. One begins to think in terms of service rather than salvation. "How can I help?" becomes a more urgent question than "How can I heal?" And this shift—though subtle—is radical. It realigns the will. It recalibrates the body. It opens the door to Hierarchy.

Alice Bailey writes that "consciousness is the response of matter to contact." This definition seems simple, but it contains within it the entire key to spiritual development. The more refined our matter—physical, emotional, and mental—the more expansive our consciousness becomes. This is not about belief systems or philosophies, but about the vibratory responsiveness of the vehicle. As the body is purified, the heart calmed, the mind stilled, we become capable of communion with broader ranges of energy. And this communion is what we call expanded consciousness.

This is why every true path requires purification—not as punishment, but as preparation. The vehicle must match the tone of the Light it seeks to embody. This is not moralism, but science. The fiery will of the Monad cannot descend into a disordered system. The soul cannot anchor in a psyche clouded by fear and fragmentation. The planes of being are ordered by law, and the expansion of consciousness is not a random bloom—it is a precisely coordinated alignment of purpose, frequency, and form.

What many seekers fail to realize is that the path of consciousness expansion includes contraction. This is the sacred tension. The heart opens, then closes. The mind stretches, then retreats. There are moments of bliss, of luminous knowing, followed by days of numbness or disillusionment. This is not regression—it is integration. The system must rewire itself. The old must be cleared. Think of the tide: it does not rise in a straight line, but in waves. You are not failing when the light recedes. You are breathing with the Universe.

The Arcane School teaches that "spiritual tension" is essential to the soul's progress. Not stress. Not strain. But a poised, directed focus—a holding of the line. This is the tension between the known and the unknown, between form and spirit. It is the tension of the bow before release. Expansion of consciousness is not always peaceful. Sometimes it is pressure. A burning behind the eyes. A sudden silence between thoughts. A pulling in the chest as though something vast is trying to emerge from within. And that is exactly what is happening.

This sacred tension demands discipline, but not rigidity. The disciple must become like tempered glass—clear and strong, but also able to yield without breaking. Rigidity fractures. But disciplined flexibility—devotion paired with discernment—creates the perfect conditions for light transmission. When your system is refined and steady, Hierarchy can work through you. You become not just a student, but a living conduit of the Plan. Your very presence becomes radiatory.

Modern seekers are now being prepared for group initiation. The days of solitary enlightenment are giving way to synthetic service—conscious collaboration with the inner government of the world. This expansion of consciousness cannot be measured by visions, emotions, or psychic display. It is measured by one's capacity to serve without ego. To radiate without attachment. To participate in the unfolding Will without resistance. That is why the trials of this era are so severe. We are being tested for coherence. For alignment. For readiness.

And yet, this is also a time of grace. Never before has there been such direct access to streams of higher energy. The veil is thinner. The Hierarchy is closer. The Soul is louder. If you are feeling stretched, pressed, emptied—it is because you are being re-formed. You are not broken. You are being made into a vessel. A chalice for new light. The expansion of consciousness is not always ecstatic. Sometimes it is silent, slow, and painful. But its fruit is permanent. Once you expand, you do not return.

Each of us contains a microcosm of this vast architecture. You are not just expanding upward—you are expanding inward and outward in every direction. The mind becomes more spacious. The heart becomes more inclusive. The will becomes more aligned. And at some point, this inner expansion births action. Not frantic effort, but sacred doing. A knowing rises from within: this is mine to do. And that knowing becomes fuel.

In your expansion, expect to lose things. Old dreams. Old desires. Old identities. This is part of the purification. It is not theft, but refinement. What remains is the diamond— the essence. You begin to see that life is not about acquisition, but offering. The self is not to be preserved, but given. And in that giving, the consciousness expands again. Infinitely.

Let me say this to you, reader-to-reader, seeker-to-seeker: you are doing this already. Even now, in the reading, in the feeling, in the quiet reflection—your field is opening. The Law of Expansion is responding. The Soul knows when it is recognized. And when it is, it speaks. And when it speaks, the Plan breathes more fully through your form.

You are not small. You are a vital cell in a great awakening. And you are not alone.

W.M.A.

The Seven Veils

Piercing the Illusions That Obscure the Soul

There is a reason so many on the path feel overwhelmed, disoriented, or painfully aware of their own fragmentation. It is not a flaw—it is a sign of transition. When the Soul begins to press forward into the foreground of consciousness, it pushes against all that obscures it. These obstructions—the distortions, attachments, inherited misperceptions—are not random. They are patterned, structured, and held in place by what occultists call the veils.

These veils are not external. They live within the fields of the personality: within mind, emotion, and body. And as you seek alignment with the higher frequencies of Light, these veils begin to burn, tremble, and eventually fall—if you are willing. Each veil is not just a block; it is also a lesson. A guardian. A mirror. To pierce them is to walk through yourself, shedding layer after layer of illusion, and revealing what has always been true.

In the teachings of C. Jinarājadāsa, these seven veils are described as the layers that prevent the soul from fully shining through. They are not evil in themselves—they are necessary sheaths, built through lifetimes. But now, in this time of rapid spiritual emergence, these veils must be confronted and transmuted if we are to serve humanity as clear vessels for the Plan.

Veil One: The Illusion of the Separated Self

This is the foundational distortion—the deeply conditioned belief that you are a self-contained, isolated being. It shows up as competitiveness, comparison, ego identification, and survival-based thinking. It tells you that you must "be someone" in order to matter. When this veil begins to dissolve, you start to sense your permeability. You are part of a field. Your actions affect the whole. Your suffering is not private. Your light is not yours alone. Realizing this is painful to the ego—but liberating to the Soul.

Veil Two: The Authority of the Outer World

This veil forms through education, media, religion, and social norms. It trains the personality to seek truth externally—through experts, institutions, or inherited beliefs. It says: Someone else knows better than you. When this veil is pierced, you reclaim the authority of your own inner knowing—not as arrogance, but as resonance. The Soul speaks quietly. To hear it, you must be willing to question what has always been "true." Discernment replaces obedience. Stillness replaces noise.

Veil Three: The False Sanctity of Suffering

Many seekers carry a hidden belief that to suffer is to be holy. That struggle is proof of spiritual depth. This veil is tricky because it masquerades as humility. But true humility is not self-denial—it is Soul-recognition. When this veil dissolves, you release the martyr. You stop glorifying your wounds. You stop identifying with pain.

Instead, you transmute it. You become a warrior of joy. Not naïve, but radiant. Not disconnected, but sovereign.

Veil Four: The Emotional Labyrinth

This is the veil of reaction, projection, and identification with emotion as identity. "I am angry. I am afraid. I am lost." In truth, you are none of these. You are the Light witnessing them. When this veil is pierced, the astral body begins to still. You feel without drowning. You express without attachment. Love becomes real—not sentimental, but stable. This veil is thinned through breath, through daily reflection, and most of all, through the cultivation of harmlessness.

Veil Five: The Mind as Master

The lower mind is useful. Brilliant, even. But it is not the throne. When this veil is active, thought loops dominate awareness. Analysis substitutes for knowing. Plans substitute for purpose. When pierced, the mind becomes a servant. Intuition rises. Space appears between thoughts. The mental body clears, like a sky after a storm. The Soul can now reflect through the mirror of the mind without distortion. It is through this veil that occult meditation becomes most powerful.

Veil Six: Fear of Power

This veil is paradoxical. Many seekers claim to seek the Light but subconsciously resist the very power they are asking for. Why? Because true spiritual power is disruptive. It will dissolve your relationships, your roles, and your comfort. It will demand that you act. When this veil falls, you no longer apologize for your clarity. You begin to wield your words as instruments of the Plan. You become magnetic—not for attention, but for service.

Veil Seven: The Illusion of Death

This final veil is the root of all fear: the belief that consciousness ends. That loss is real. That identity can be erased. But when this veil dissolves—often through direct mystical experience or deep soul revelation—you awaken to the Infinite. You realize you are not the wave, but the ocean expressing itself uniquely. You no longer cling. You no longer panic. You serve with a calm that is unshakable. Life and death become doors, not opposites. The Soul becomes you.

To pierce these veils is not a single event. It is a process. A spiral. One veil falls, then returns, then falls again more fully. This is why the path demands patience. This is why grace is so important. You are not failing if the old illusions come back—you are refining. Shedding. Burning what remains.

Occult meditation is the most powerful tool for this process. Not to escape life, but to anchor the Soul into it.

It teaches the personality to yield. It sharpens the will, aligns the heart, clears the mind. And in time, it becomes the temple through which the Solar Angel radiates. This is no metaphor. This is spiritual physics.

As Jinarājadāsa writes:

"Each veil is a necessary illusion, shattered only when the light within burns brighter than the world around."

And so your task is not to force awakening, but to feed the flame. Study. Reflect. Choose silence. Speak truth. Walk in harmlessness. Love without ownership. Meditate the Plan into form.

The world needs clear souls now. Not perfect. Not pure. But willing.

You do not need to know everything. You do not need to see the end.
You only need to hold the thread of light—through the fog, through the flame—until the next step appears.

And as each veil dissolves, the Soul shines a little brighter. The mind stills a little more. The heart widens. And the Light, at last, has a vessel.

W.M.A

CHAPTER VI

ALCHEMICAL TRANSMUTATION AND ITS PROCESSES

*"Within the crucible of the Self, all elements are refined
—until gold remembers it was always Light."*

The Masters Speak

There are moments on the Path when everything begins to dissolve—and we are tempted to believe something has gone wrong. But what is actually occurring is the sacred, painful, glorious process of transmutation. The fire has arrived. And it has come to burn away all that is no longer aligned with who we are becoming.

Transmutation is not gentle. It is not kind in the way we usually think of kindness. It is an act of divine exactness— a confrontation with everything that resists Light, both within and around us. It is the force that compels the personality to yield to the Soul, the ego to step aside for the flame of Purpose.

The alchemist does not fear the burn. The true initiate calls for it—though they know the price. Because they understand that this fire is not a punishment. It is a passage. A reconstitution of essence. A re-ordering of all internal architecture to align with something vaster, cleaner, and infinitely more beautiful.

We have each walked through fire in our own way. Whether through crisis, initiation, illness, or awakening— we know what it feels like to lose the ground beneath us and to find, beneath that loss, a deeper foundation rising. This is what the Ageless Wisdom calls the burning ground —a space between what was and what will be, where only truth survives.

And so this chapter begins not with a technique, but with a truth:

You will be changed.
You will not emerge the same. And that is the point.

You are not here to patch the old. You are here to become the new.
And that becoming is made possible only through fire.

In the pages that follow, we will explore the occult understanding of transmutation—not as metaphor, but as energetic law. You will hear the voices of the Masters, of the Old Commentary, of the fire itself. And then we will walk together through what it means to live this process fully, consciously, and with grace.

So take a breath.
Feel into your body.
And if you are ready,
step into the crucible.

W.M.A

The Philosopher's Stone and the Inner Fire

You already contain the alchemical ingredients.
This cannot be emphasized enough.

The goal of the alchemist—spoken in riddles, guarded in glyphs, buried in stone—is not to create gold, but to become it. The Philosopher's Stone, long sought through chemistry and secrecy, is not outside of you. It is within. And it is formed not in the lab, but in the Soul.

The ancient texts called it the lapis philosophorum, the Stone of the Wise. But wisdom does not mean information. It means integration. The true Philosopher's Stone is forged through the transmutation of base matter —fear, pride, lust, doubt—into refined substance: clarity, will, love, and light. This is not symbolic. It is energetic science. And it happens inside your own body and consciousness, layer by sacred layer.

You are the vessel.
The ingredients are your experiences.
The fire is your Soul.
And the Stone is what emerges when all has been burned but truth.

This process cannot be rushed, but it can be recognized. You will know you are forming the Stone when your reactions begin to soften. When your clarity deepens. When your identity detaches from personality and begins to root in Presence. When you feel the flame inside you burning steadily—not in flashes, but in rhythm. These are signs that the alchemical work is well underway.

There are stages, yes—Calcination, Dissolution, Separation, Conjunction, Fermentation, Distillation, and Coagulation—as the classical mystics taught. But more important than memorizing the map is knowing where you are on it. Are you still burning through attachments? Dissolving illusions? Distilling what is essential? Or are you beginning to feel the quiet weight of something new —something solid—crystallizing inside you?

That is the Stone.

The Philosopher's Stone is not a destination. It is a function. A capacity. Once formed, it allows you to hold the Fire without being consumed. It grants you the power of transmutation—not through effort, but through presence. Others feel it when they are near you. Systems reconfigure themselves around you. Doors open—not because you force them, but because your vibration unlocks them.

And yet, even this is only the beginning.

For those who continue—who walk with reverence and precision—there comes a greater revelation: that the inner Stone, when perfectly formed, becomes a key to perceiving the outer Stone. What some call the Materia Lucida—the Light Substance. The physical Philosopher's Stone. Not made, but found. Not invented, but uncovered. Not through laboratories, but through lifetimes of refinement.

This is not fantasy.

It is mystery.
And mystery is only secrecy until the Soul is ready.
So let this be your encouragement:
You are already in the Work.
You are already in possession of the raw materials.
You are already becoming the flame that reveals the Stone.

And if you are reading these words, then the fire is close—perhaps already burning.

Ψ

Introduction to the Great Work

The "Great Work," or *Magnum Opus,* is one of the most enduring and mysterious symbols within the Western esoteric tradition, alchemy, and the Ageless Wisdom teachings. Veiled in cryptic language by medieval and Renaissance alchemists, and spiritually reframed by modern occultists, this phrase does not refer to the literal transmutation of base metals into gold, but rather to the inner process of spiritual refinement—the transmutation of the lower self into a radiant vessel of divine purpose. It is the path by which a human being becomes a soul-infused being and, ultimately, an instrument of the divine Will.

In esoteric psychology, the Great Work signifies the process by which the personality is purified and unified, then aligned with the Soul, and eventually fused with the higher spiritual triad. In the words of the *Secret Doctrine,* "Man is that being in whom Spirit and Matter meet." The Magnum Opus is the conscious path of reconciling these apparent opposites.

It is also the fulfillment of the universal promise made by every ancient wisdom tradition: that humanity may rise, not only through devotion or worship, but through knowledge, discipline, and transformation. As H.P. Blavatsky writes, "There is no religion higher than truth," and it is truth—seen, lived, and embodied—that the Great Work aims to reveal. The reward for those who take up this inner labor is not personal glorification, but greater capacity for service, deeper clarity, and entrance into the stream of hierarchical and planetary evolution.

Like the steps on the Path of Initiation, the Great Work unfolds in distinct yet overlapping stages. These stages— commonly known as Nigredo, Albedo, Citrinitas, and Rubedo—describe the transmutation of consciousness through dissolution, purification, illumination, and integration. Though these stages were originally presented in metaphorical or chemical terms, they are deeply relevant to the spiritual aspirant.

What follows is a modern esoteric reflection on each of these phases, presented as a guide to seekers working consciously toward spiritual integration and planetary service. These stages are designed for one to move them repetitively through their lives as need. The Magnum Opus is a practice. With time, the **Stone** will brighten and the occult secret of immortality will reveal itself.

The Magnum Opus of the Soul

In the esoteric traditions, both Western and Eastern, the path of inner transformation has often been described through the symbolic framework of alchemy. Beyond the surface interpretation of turning base metals into gold, true alchemy is the science of spiritual transmutation. The "Magnum Opus," or the Great Work, refers to the elevation of the human condition into divine expression. It is the conscious refinement of the lower self, the uniting of opposites, and the realization of the Self as Spirit-in-form.

The stages of the Great Work have been articulated in many ways, but most classical Hermetic and Rosicrucian systems present four principal phases: **Nigredo** (Blackening), **Albedo** (Whitening), **Citrinitas** (Yellowing), and **Rubedo**(Reddening). Each phase has spiritual, psychological, and energetic parallels, and these can be applied to the path of the seeker, the disciple, and the initiate alike.

Nigredo: The Blackening

This is the phase of dissolution, death, and darkness. It is often triggered by a crisis, a loss, or a profound confrontation with the shadow self. In modern psychological terms, it resembles the dark night of the soul. The old structures break down. The seeker realizes the inadequacy of the personality-centered life, and the soul begins to stir behind the veil of suffering.

In this stage, all that is impure, false, or fragmented within the self is exposed. From the Theosophical and Agni Yoga perspectives, this is the confrontation with the Dweller on the Threshold. Meditation, reflection, and psychological honesty are the keys to passing through Nigredo with integrity. Though painful, this stage is vital. It is where the fire is kindled.

Practical Application: Allow yourself to sit with your discomfort. Journal your thoughts, acknowledge your patterns, and engage in regular meditation. Observe without judgment. The putrefaction is not a failure—it is the necessary breakdown of the old self to make way for the Soul.

Albedo: The Whitening

After the dissolution comes the washing. Albedo is the stage of purification. It is associated with the rising light of the Soul, the flooding in of clarity and purpose. Often described as the time of "illumination," it is here that the aspirant begins to see the outlines of spiritual reality more clearly.

In the Arcane School, this is the period in which the disciple begins to achieve mental control and alignment. The lower self becomes more responsive to the higher. The waters of emotion are calmed. Many aspirants begin to receive intuitive insights and synchronistic guidance.

This is also a phase of detachment. Having seen the illusions and glamour for what they are, the disciple now begins to purify the mind and emotions. It is a time of cleansing, of re-ordering one's life, and of serving from a place of growing selflessness.

Practical Application: Focus on aligning with your Soul through meditation and study. Simplify your environment. Practice harmlessness in thought, word, and deed. This is the time for inner discipline and humility.

Citrinitas: The Yellowing

Though sometimes omitted in simplified descriptions, Citrinitas is essential. It is the dawn before the full sunrise. This phase represents integration and the beginning of wisdom. Here, the purified elements of the personality begin to come into creative harmony with the Soul. The mind becomes illuminated by intuition, and the will-to-good emerges more fully.

In esoteric Christianity, this is symbolized by the transfiguration. In Hermeticism, it is the birth of the Philosopher's Child. This is the time when the true magnetic aura begins to radiate. The disciple is no longer seeking enlightenment—they are becoming a light-bearer.

Practical Application: Seek balance between contemplation and action. Begin teaching or sharing your insights as a form of service. Align yourself with a spiritual group or school if you haven't already. Focus on integration—not perfection.

Rubedo: The Reddening

This is the final phase of the Work. It represents illumination, the descent of the spirit fully into matter. The purified and aligned personality becomes a vehicle for the Monad via the Soul. The Fire of Spirit is now fully grounded in the world through the initiate.

Rubedo is the stage of joy, of radiant compassion, of the Christed consciousness manifesting in daily life. The red symbolizes not only vitality and passion, but the sacrificial blood—the willingness to serve, to give one's life to the higher purposes of the Plan.

This is the time of Initiation. In the language of the Ageless Wisdom, the Soul has fulfilled its task of integration and begins to disintegrate, that the Monad may shine through without obstruction.

Practical Application: Live simply. Serve greatly. Abide in silence when needed, and speak only that which furthers the Plan. Radiate the fire of joy without needing recognition. Embody the truths you've come to know.

The Living Flame

The Great Work is not metaphorical—it is literal. It is the daily, hourly task of bringing light into form, of transforming suffering into wisdom, of refining the dense into the luminous. Though clothed in ancient language, it is the work of every sincere aspirant. Each stage is part of a spiral that repeats, deepens, and expands.

Through occult meditation, service, study, and sacrifice, we undertake the alchemical marriage within ourselves, until there is no longer a separation between spirit and form. We become fire itself, walking the Earth with eyes that see and hearts that serve.

This is the purpose of Alchemical Transmutation. This is the Great Work. And it begins wherever you are, in this very moment.

Before we step forward, let us now turn our attention to the ancient wisdom that underpins this entire process. In the pages that follow, you will encounter teachings drawn from A Treatise on Cosmic Fire, where the foundational postulates of occult transmutation are revealed—veiled in language that is precise, paradoxical, and deeply symbolic. Do not rush through them. Read slowly. Let the words open within you. The Old Commentary was never meant to be digested at the surface; it is a key that turns only when your own fire begins to match the vibration of the truths it contains. Read as a student, but also as a living flame. What you recognize in these words... is what you are already becoming.

W.M.A

Excerpt
A Treatise on Cosmic Fire
A.A.B.

In defining transmutation as it is occultly understood, we might express it thus: *Transmutation is the passage across from one state of being to another through the agency of fire.* The due comprehension of this is based on certain postulates, mainly four in number. These postulates must be expressed in terms of the Old Commentary, which is so worded that it reveals to those who have eyes to see, but remains enigmatic to those who are not ready, or who would misuse the knowledge gained for selfish ends. The phrases are as follows:

I.

He who transfers the the Father's life to the lower three seeketh the agency of fire, hid in the heart of the Mother. He worketh with the Agnichaitans, that hide, that burn, and thus produce the needed moisture.

II

He who transfers the life from out the lower three into the ready fourth seeketh the agency of fire hid in the heart of Brahma. He worketh with the forces of the Agnishvattas, that emanate, that blend, and thus produce the needed warmth.

III

He who transfers the life into the gathering fifth seeketh the agency of fire hid in the heart of Vishnu. He worketh with the forces of the Agnisuryans, that blaze, that liberate the essence, and thus produce the needed radiance.

First moisture, slow and all enveloping; then heat with ever-growing warmth and fierce intensity; then force that presses, drives and concentrates. Thus is radiance produced; thus the exudation; thus mutation; thus change of form. Finally liberation, escape of the volatile essence, and the gather of the residue back to primordial stuff.

One who ponders these formulas and who meditates upon the method and suggested process will receive a general idea of the evolutionary process of transmutation which will be of more value to him than the formulas whereby the devas transmute the various minerals.

Transmutation concerns the life of the atom, and is hidden in a knowledge of the laws governing radioactivity. It is interesting to note how in the scientific expression 'radioactivity,' we have the eastern conception of Vishnu-Brahma, or the Rays of Light vibrating through matter. Hence the usually accepted interpretation of the term 'atom' must be extended from that of the atom of chemistry to include:

a. All atoms or spheres upon the physical plane.
b. All atoms or spheres upon the astral and mental planes.
c. The human being in physical incarnation.
d. The causal body of man on its own plane.
e. All planes as entified spheres.
f. All planets, chains and globes within the solar system.
g. All monads on their own plane, whether human monads or Heavenly Men.

h. The solar Ring-Pass-Not, the aggregate of all lesser
    atoms.

In all these atoms, stupendous or minute, microcosmic or
macrocosmic, the central life corresponds to the positive
charge of electrical force predicated by science, whether it
is the life of a cosmic Entity such as a solar Logos, or the
tiny elemental life within a physical atom. The lesser
atoms which revolve around their positive center, and
which are at present termed electrons by science, are the
negative aspect, and this is true not only of the atom on
the physical plane, but of the human atoms, half to their
central attractive point, a Heavenly Man, or the atomic
forms which in their aggregate form the recognized solar
system.

The second point I seek to make now isL *Radiation is
transmutation in process of accomplishment.* Transmutation
being the liberation of the essence in order that it may
seek a new centre, the process may be recognized as
radioactivity technically understood and applied to all
atomic bodies without exception.

{Radium is an example for us of the process of
transmutation}

As this is more comprehended it will be found that all
radiations, such as magnetism or psychic exhalation, are
but the transmuting process proceeding on a large scale.
The point to be grasped here is that the transmuting
process, when effective, is superficially the result of
outside factors. Basically it is the result of the inner
positive nucleus of force or life reaching such a terrific
rate of vibration, that it eventually scatters the electrons

or negative points which compose its sphere of influence, and scatters them to such a distance that the Law of Repulsion, and the central essence escapes and seeks a new sphere, occultly understood.

We must remember always that all within the solar system is dual, and is in itself both negative and positive: positive as regards its own form, but negative as regards its greater sphere. Every atom therefore is both positive and negative,— it is an electron as well as an atom.

Therefore, the process of transmutation is dual and necessitates a preliminary stage of application of external factors, a fanning and care and development of the inner positive nucleus, a period of incubation or of the systematic feeding of the inner flame, and an increase of voltage. There is next a secondary stage wherein the external factors do not count so much, and wherein the inner center of energy in the atom may be left to do its own work. These factors may be applied equally to all atoms; to the mineral atoms which have occupied attention of alchemists so much, to the atom, called man who pursues the same general procedure being governed by the same laws; and to all greater atoms, such as Heavenly Man or a solar Logos.

The process might be tabulated as follows:

1. The life takes primitive form.
2. The form is subjected to outer heat.
3. Heat, playing on the form, produces exudation and the factor of moisture supervenes.
4. Moisture and heat perform their function in unison.
5. Elemental lives tend all lesser lives.
6. The devas cooperate under rule, order and sound.
7. The internal heat of the atom increases.
8. The heat of the atom mounts rapidly and surpasses the external heat of its environing.
9. The atom radiates.
10. The spheroidal wall of the atom is eventually broken down.
11. The electrons or negative units seek a new center.
12. The central life escapes to merge with its polar opposite becoming itself negative and seeking the positive.
13. This is occultly obscuration, the going-out of the light temporarily, until it again emerges and blazes forth.

More detailed elucidation will not be possible here nor advisable.

It will be apparent, therefore, that is should be possible, from the standpoint of each kingdom of nature, to aid the transmuting process of all lesser atoms. This is so, even though it is not recognized; it is only when the human kingdom is reached that it is possible for an entity consciously and intelligently to do two things:

First: aid in the transmutation of his own positive atomic center from the human into the spiritual.

Second: assist at the transmutation
   a. From the lower mineral forms into higher forms.
   b. From the mineral forms into the vegetable.
   c. From vegetable forms into the animal forms.
   d. From animal forms into the human or consciously and definitely to bring about individualization.

That it is not done as yet is due to the danger of imparting the necessary knowledge. The adepts understand the transmuting process in the three worlds, and in the four kingdoms of nature, which make them a temporary esoteric three and exoteric four.

Man will eventually work with the three kingdoms but, only when brotherhood is a practice and not a concept.

Three points must now be considered in this connection:

   Conscious manipulations of the fires.
   Devas and transmutation.
   Sound and color in transmutation.

It is necessary here to point out, as I have done in other matters under consideration, that only certain facts can be imparted, whilst the detailed work concerning *process* may not be dealt with owing to the inability of the human race as yet to act altruistically. Much misapprehension crept in, owing to this very thing, in the early days of hierarchical effort to give out some of the Wisdom fundamentals in book form...The danger still persists, and greatly handicaps the efforts of Those, Who—working on the inner side—feel that the thoughts of men should be lifted from the study of the ways of physical existence to broader concepts, wider vision, and synthetic comprehension.

Indication is only possible; it is not permissible here to give out the transmutative formulas, or the mantrams that manipulate the matter of space. Only the way can be pointed to those who are ready, or who are recovering old knowledge (gained through approach to the Path, or latent through experience undergone in Atlantean days) and the land marks indicated hold sufficient guidance to enable them to penetrate deeper into the arcana of knowledge.

The danger consists in the very fact that the whole matter of transmutation concerns the material form, and deva substance. Man, being not yeet master even of the substance of his own sheaths, nor in vibratory control of his third aspect, incurs risk when he concentrates his attention on the Not-Self.

It can only be safely done when the magician knows five things:

I

The true nature of the atom.

II

The keynote of the planes.

III

The method of workin from the egoic level through conscious control, knowledge of the protective sounds and formulas, and pure altruistic endeavor.

IV

The interaction of the three fires, the lunar words, the solar words, and later a cosmic word.

V

The secret of electrical vibration, which is only realized in an elementary way when a man knows the keynote of his own planetary Logos.

All this knowledge as it concerns the three worlds is in the hands of the Masters of the Wisdom, and enables Them to work along the lines of energy or force, and not with what is usually understood when the word 'substance' is used. They work with electrical energy, concerning Themselves with positive electricity, or with the energy of the positive nucleus of force within the atom, whether it is the atom of chemistry, for instance, or the human atom. They *deal with the soul of things.*

The black magician works with the negative aspect, with the electrons, if I might so term it, with the sheath and not with the soul. This distinction must be clearly borne in mind. It holds the clue to the non-interference of the whole Brotherhood in material matters and affairs, and Their concentration upon the *force* aspect, upon the centers of energy.

They reach the whole through the agency of the few centers in a form.

With this preamble we will now take up the consideration of the—

Conscious Manipulation of the Fires

It will now be apparent that the whole process of transmutation, as we can deal with it at present, concerns itself with the two fires which reached a high stage of perfection in a past solar system:

a. The fire of an atom in its twofold aspect—internal and radiatory.

b. The fires of mind.

It is with these that transmutation concerns itself from the human standpoint, and the third fire of Spirit is not at this stage to be considered.

This *conscious* manipulation of the fires is the prerogative of man when he has reached a certain point in his evolution; the unconscious realization of this has led naturally to the attempts of the alchemist to transmute in the mineral kingdom. A few of the older students right through the ages have comprehended the vastness of the endeavour of which the transmutation of the baser metals into gold was but preliminary and a symbol, a pictorial, allegorical, concrete step.

The whole subject of transmutation is covered by the work of the Hierarchy in all its three departments on this planet, and we might get some idea of the matters involved if we studied this vast hierarchical standpoint, getting thereby a concept of the work done in aiding the evolutionary process. It is the work of transferring the life from one stage of atomic existence to another, and it involves three distinct steps, which can be seen and traced by means of the higher clairvoyance, and from the higher planes. These steps or stages are:

The Fiery Stage—the blending, fusing, burning period, through which all atoms pass during the disintegration of form.

The Solvent Stage—in which the form is dissipated and substance is held in solution, the atom being resolved into its essential duality.

The Volatile Stage—which concerns primarily the essential quality of the atom, and the escape of this essence, later to take a new form.

Radioactivity, pralayic solution, and essential volatility might express the thought. In every transmuting process without exception these three steps are followed. Occultly expressed in the Old Commentary, they are thus stated:

> "The fiery lives burn within the bosom of the Mother.
> The fiery center extends to the periphery of the circle and dissipation supervenes and pralayic peace.
> The Son returns to the bosom of the Father, and Mother rests quiescent."

The master, in concert with the great Devas, concern Themselves with this transmutative process, and each department might be considered as dealing with one of the three stages:

The Mahachohan's department in its five divisions deals with the burning of the fiery lives.

The Manu's department concerns itself with the form or the ring-pass-not which encloses the burning lives.

The Bodhisattva's department deals with the return of the Son to the bosom of the Father.

Within the department of the Mahachohan, a secondary division along these lives might be outlined:

The seventh and fifth Rays are occupied with the return of the Son to the Father and are largely centered in pouring forth energizing power when it becomes necessary to transfer the life of the Son from an old form into a new, from one kingdom of nature to another on the Path of Return.

The third and sixth Rays deal with the burning of the fiery lives.

The fourth blends the two fires within the atomic form.

It will be seen from a close study of these subdivisions, how close is the cooperation between the different groups, and how interrelated are their activities. The work of the Hierarchy can be interpreted always in terms of alchemy, and Their activities deal with a threefold transmutation. The work is carried on by Them *consciously*, and supervenes upon Their own emancipation.

A *Master* transmutes in the three worlds and principally concerns Himself with the process upon the eighteen sub planes, the great field of human evolution, and with the passage of the life throughout the dense physical body of the Logos. *The Chohans* of the sixth initiation work in the fourth and fifth ethers of the logoic etheric body (the buddhic and atmic planes), and deal with the passage of the life of Spirit from form to form in those worlds, having in view the transmutation of units in the spiritual kingdom of the monadic. Those on still higher levels— *the Buddhas and their Confreres of the first and third Rays*—deal with the passage of the life into the subatomic, and atomic planes of the cosmic physical.

What has been said applies to all Hierarchical efforts in all schemes and on all globes, for the unity of effort is universal. In every case, conscious self-induced control, or authority, precedes ability to transmute. *Initiates* learn to transmute and superintend the passage of the life out of the animal kingdom into the human after the third Initiation, and during the earlier stages of initiation, formulas that control the lesser devas, and which produce results in the merging of the second and third kingdoms are communicated; they work under safeguards and supervision.

Advanced intellectual man should be able to cooperate in the synthesis of the work, and deal with the transmutation of the metals, as the ratio of their intellectual development to that of the mineral elements, and builders whom they would control, is the same as in the above mentioned cases and grades of consciousness, but owing to the disastrous developments in Atlantean days, and the consequent stultification of spiritual evolution for a time until karma has been adjusted, the art has been lost; or rather, the knowledge has been safeguarded until a period is reached in the racial progress wherein the physical body is pure enough to withstand the forces contacted, and to emerge from the process of chemical transmutation enriched, not only in knowledge and experience, but strengthened in it own fibre.

A Treatise on Cosmic Fire
A.A.B.

After the Fire: The Expansion Begins

You have just read a passage whose density is its own kind of fire.

Do not be discouraged if your mind did not grasp every concept in linear sequence. These teachings are not meant to be consumed passively—they are initiatory, catalytic, and transmutative. They are encoded in flame.

To study A Treatise on Cosmic Fire is to open oneself to the threefold fire that underlies all existence:

•   The Fire of Matter (kundalini, the latent heat at the base of form)

•   The Fire of the Soul (solar fire, or the radiance of the causal body)

•   The Fire of Spirit (electric fire, the will of the Monad expressed through Purpose)

These are not just metaphysical concepts.

They are living realities within you, waiting to be recognized and worked with—safely, reverently, and with full understanding that transmutation is not gentle. It is fiery death followed by sacred rebirth. It is what turns the aspirant into a disciple, the disciple into the initiate, and the initiate into one who no longer seeks, but serves.

This is why we say:

Transmutation is not change. It is passage.

Not mere improvement—but the passage across a threshold, a burning bridge between who you have been and who your Soul demands you become.

To make this crossing, one must invoke the Fire within.

That Fire begins in the mind, not the emotions.
This is the first misunderstanding that must be cleared. Too many seekers believe transformation is a feeling, a catharsis, a moment of emotional rupture. But real transmutation begins in the act of alignment—when the mind is illumined, the emotions are stilled, and the body becomes a transmitter of higher frequency. This is the work of occult meditation. This is the method of the Soul.

We do not wait to be changed.
We participate in the burning.

As you now continue through this chapter, we will expand upon the postulates you have just encountered—bringing ancient truths into new light, grounding cosmic abstraction in lived reality, and offering practices, principles, and perspectives that will support your own journey through the Fires of Transmutation.

Together, let us approach the Philosopher's Stone within.
Together, let us build the crucible.

W.M.A

Transmutation and the Fire of Becoming
Section I

Transmutation, in the deepest occult sense, is not merely a change in substance—it is a reordering of essence. It is the internal combustion by which the personality relinquishes its hold and the Soul begins to burn its way into matter. This process is not metaphor. It is biological, energetic, and planetary.

The passage you have just read from A Treatise on Cosmic Fire offers a scaffolding of thought so high and subtle that it often stuns the intellect into silence. But let that be the first key: real spiritual knowledge is not always comprehended at first by the lower mind. It is absorbed, digested, and re-revealed in cycles. The Fire of Truth does not always arrive in sentences. Sometimes it arrives as a shiver down the spine, or a knowing in the blood, or a pause between breaths that shifts your whole trajectory.

This is how the fire begins to take root.

The passage across—from one state of being to another—requires more than aspiration. It requires the full cooperation of the mental, emotional, and physical vehicles. Transmutation demands that you become a living crucible. You must prepare your field to hold greater voltages of energy. The Light you call in will break you if your foundation is not strong. Therefore, we begin with the first fire:

The Fire of Matter: Kundalini and the Root Flame

The fire of matter is coiled in every human being.
Called kundalini in the East, this is not merely a mythic energy—it is an electrical reservoir stored in the base center, latent in most, partially awakened in some, and dangerously misused by many.

To awaken this fire safely, one must first be committed to harmlessness.
Not just emotional gentleness—but the exact alignment of will, motive, and method in service to something beyond the self. This is the fire that animates your body, that rises when the Soul descends. It is not meant to be provoked through force or thrill-seeking. That is the path of glamour. Of disaster.

The fire of matter is the lowest octave of the Divine Flame.
It is the first gatekeeper.
It tests your grounding, stability, and purity of intention.

Without these, the higher fires will never safely ignite.

The Fire of the Soul: Solar Radiance and the Causal Flame

When you are ready—when your thought life is ordered, your emotional field clarified, and your body stilled through service—then the second fire descends.

Solar fire.

The fire of the causal body.

The radiance of your Soul—not metaphorically, but electrically—beginning to penetrate the veils of the personality.

This is when things begin to change rapidly.

Synchronicities accelerate. Time dilates. Your voice, your thoughts, your magnetism begins to shift. You will begin to attract those in need of the Light you carry—and, likewise, those who resist it. This is a test of your vibration. Will you flinch? Will you contract? Or will you hold your alignment under pressure?

The Soul, once anchored, does not tolerate pretense. It burns through falsity. It demands purification. This is why the Path of Return is also called the Path of Fire. It is not safe. It is not soft. It is sacred.

And it is glorious.

The Fire of Spirit: Monad, Will, and Electric Flame

Few reach this threshold consciously in one lifetime. But the seed of it lies in every disciple. The third fire—Electric Fire—is the Fire of Spirit, the breath of the Monad. It is not an experience of light, but of Power. Not power over others, but the Power to See clearly and to Act correctly under Law.

This fire reorients the entire being.

The Will is no longer personal. The choices you make are no longer about your comfort or even your growth. They are about the exact service your Soul agreed to render before incarnation. This is when the disciple becomes an Initiate, and the Initiate becomes an Agent of the Plan.

To speak of the Monad is to speak of God—not a god outside of you, but the Flame of your essential being as it exists within the Heart of the One.

Few can endure this flame in full, but all are called toward it.

Alchemy, the Philosopher's Stone, and the Materia Lucida

The alchemical legends spoke of the Philosopher's Stone— the mysterious substance said to transmute base metals into gold. What they truly spoke of was this:

The personality (base metal) refined through fire,
Reforged by the Soul (silver),
Made into Gold through the descent of Spirit.

This is the inner Philosopher's Stone.
It is built, not found.
And it is constructed through years—lifetimes—of right living, study, meditation, and sacred trial.

Materia Lucida—the subtle substrate of all physical forms, the shining thread between atoms and stars—is the substance through which transmutation unfolds. And it is not a myth. It is the living etheric web of Divinity. It is what vibrates between you and every other Soul. It is the field of Becoming, and the canvas on which the Plan is painted.

The Stone lives in you already.

Your job is to bring it forth through right heat, right light, and right tension.

The Tests of the Fire

With each fire comes a trial:
- The fire of matter tests desire. Will you fall for power? Sensation? Possession?
- The fire of the Soul tests emotion. Will you burn away glamour? False empathy? Spiritual pride?
- The fire of Spirit tests will. Will you renounce your preferences for Purpose?

These are not theoretical questions. They arise daily in your choices.
And they must be passed repeatedly—not once, but rhythmically—until your vibration can withstand higher voltage.

This is why occult meditation is not optional on the Path. It is a scientific necessity.

The Group Crucible and the New Alchemy

In ages past, alchemy was practiced in secret. One seeker. One lab. One flame.

But today, the new alchemy is group work.

The Soul now seeks outlets in collective formation— triangles, groups, circles of service. The higher initiations are now being anchored not by individuals, but by groups aligned in love, mind, and purpose.

You are not meant to walk this Path alone.

There are those already magnetized to your frequency. And as you transmute yourself, your field will pull them into orbit. Likewise, you will find yourself pulled into higher groups, where greater flames await.

Becoming the Flame

Transmutation is not the end.
It is the beginning of service.

When you cross the threshold, you do not walk into bliss. You walk into utility. You become a vessel. An agent. A willing participant in the radiation of Light into darkened places.

You become what Blavatsky called a "lamp on the path."
Not to be worshipped.
But to be used.

Let this fire burn in you until you recognize it was always yours.

Let it consume your illusion until only truth remains.

Let it illuminate the next page, the next prayer, the next step.

Because from here, beloved seeker…
You do not go back.

Transmutation and the Fire of Becoming
Section II

To transmute is to suffer consciously, to suffer wisely, and to emerge radiant. This truth may be clothed in metaphor, but its process is exact, scientific, and spiritual all at once. The sacred alchemy that has long been hidden in code and symbol is now, in this era of awakening, being rediscovered in the human body itself.

The glandular system, the nervous system, and the subtle energy bodies are not separate from this work—they are its laboratory. The ancient phrase *solve et coagula*—to dissolve and to bind—applies not just to metals but to thoughts, emotions, identities. The alchemist of today must learn to dissolve inherited glamours, karmic residues, and egoic fixations into the fires of dispassion, and then rebind the purified essence into a vehicle fit for service.

The **pituitary and pineal glands**, when awakened through aligned spiritual practice, form an energetic arc across the brain—sometimes referred to as the *light bridge* or the *rainbow bridge*. As the currents intensify, this bridge facilitates the descent of solar fire into the personality vehicle, allowing higher impressions to be registered with clarity and stability. The heart center, when magnetized, distributes this energy to the etheric body, reconfiguring its vibration. The result is a luminous aura, capable of both shielding and transmitting.

But none of this occurs in a vacuum. It occurs in the crucible of the world.

Modern transmutation happens not in monasteries, but in grief. In heartbreak. In breakdowns and breakthroughs. It is in the pain of injustice, the silence after death, the moment of shame or fear or exposure that you would have once run from, but now choose to stand within— *with eyes open*. These are the new cauldrons. This is the fire.

When initiates speak of karma, they do not speak of punishment. They speak of opportunity—*the heat needed to awaken latent substance*. The Lead is not your sin. The Lead is your material. Your failures, your pride, your old programming—these are what you are here to alchemize. You are not meant to discard them. You are meant to cook them.

Transmutation is not linear, nor is it clean. It comes in spirals, reversals, reactivations. You may think yourself through a layer of fire, only to be plunged back in months or years later from a higher turn. This is not failure. It is deeper refinement. It is the Soul shaping its instrument with exacting love.

And yet there is joy. Unspeakable joy.

The lightness that arises from a transmuted wound is unlike any bliss the personality has ever known. It does not exalt. It humbles. It leaves you wanting to bow to the smallest things—a leaf, a breath, a stranger's laughter. This is the golden state. Not triumph. Not grandeur. But sacred usefulness. A body purified to radiate. A mind fit to reflect. A heart stable enough to burn without harm.

What happens when a soul reaches this state?

They become a transmitter.

Every thought begins to shape the ether. Every breath begins to ripple into fields unknown. And every act, however small, becomes a **ceremony of consecration**. This is the real magic. Not spellwork, not performance— but vibration, presence, and right alignment with Hierarchy. The white magician does not declare. The white magician radiates.

In this sense, your life becomes an invocation. Your presence becomes a talisman.

This is where the path of service begins—not when you are healed, but when you are willing to offer even your healing process to the Plan. Even your grief. Even your unknowing. Especially your unknowing. For in the spaciousness of not-knowing, the higher impressions can at last be received.

And what of Earth herself?

She too is undergoing transmutation.

The entire planetary Logos is passing through initiation. Humanity is the throat center of this great planetary being, and it is through our collective expression, speech, and thought that Earth finds her voice within the solar system. As we refine our own vehicles, we assist in the refinement of Hers.

The fires of climate, conflict, and collapse are not signs of doom—they are signs of crisis, which in its root meaning is a *decision point*. We are in the furnace. Will we turn to the Plan? Will we serve the Whole? Or will we resist the fire and be shattered?

Discipleship is not optional anymore. It is a planetary necessity.

So let the fires come. Let them burn through fear, through illusion, through separation. You are not here to be safe. You are here to be refined. And through you—*through your transmutation*—the Light of the future will find form.

Transmutation and the Fire of Becoming
Section III

What emerges from fire is not merely warmth or light—it is **essence**, clarified. The alchemical metaphor becomes reality when we understand that the Soul itself is a furnace. It distills our lifetimes, our karma, our inherited patterns, and reveals in time the diamond core.

Each act of purification, each meditation that realigns us to the Source, contributes to the stabilization of that diamond structure within. The Master within—the Solar Angel—does not sculpt you through comfort. It refines you through pressure, intention, and radiant love.

As we proceed deeper into the Aquarian era, transmutation will become more collective. We are already seeing the outer signs: group initiations, mass awakenings, and simultaneous recognitions of spiritual responsibility across continents and cultures. The Soul of Humanity is **sounding its chord**—and those whose cords are in tune are responding.

The next stage, therefore, is to become **an instrument of that chord**.

To do so, we must let go of the glamour of personal enlightenment. There is no individual graduation. No final "ascension" that removes us from the field. True transmutation initiates us into deeper responsibility—not escape. As the fire purifies us, we are invited not to float above the Earth, but to **anchor Heaven into it**.

This is why the Ageless Wisdom has returned in waves through the teachings of H.P. Blavatsky, Alice Bailey, Helena Roerich, and many others. This is why esotericism is no longer hidden behind locked doors. Because we have reached the threshold where the *Group Soul* must awaken, and only through shared service and shared vision will the fire be contained and consecrated.

We are becoming sacred architecture. We are laying etheric bricks and summoning Ray builders. We are crafting **living temples of resonance** that will stand long after these bodies are gone.

The fire asks only one question: **Will you allow yourself to be changed?**

Not improved. Not perfected. But **reborn**.

Let that answer ripple into your actions. Let your meditations become fire chambers. Let your thoughts be rituals, your friendships be initiations, your creativity be combustion.

And let your life—however ordinary or extraordinary it may seem—become the very path of transmutation itself.

You are the crucible. You are the fire. You are the gold.

And this Work, beloved, has only just begun.

"The Flame becomes the Fire. The Fire becomes the Light. The Light becomes the Path."

Invocation of the Living Flame

O Flame within the Heart of my Being,
You who know the Blueprint of my becoming,
Ignite in me the Will to serve, the Light to see, the Love to
stand steady in the storm.

I offer up all that is unrefined.
I surrender the lead of fear, shame, pride, and illusion.
I give it to the Fire of the Soul, that it may be recast in
Truth.

By the power of Sacred Fire,
By the breath of the Solar Angel,
By the call of the Monad,
May I be shaped into usefulness.

May my thoughts be radiant.
May my speech be precise.
May my body become a chalice of Light.

Let the fires that pass through me become Light for others.
Let the radiance of my being serve the Plan,
And let the silence in my soul resound with the Name of
the One.

I am the Fire.
I am the Flame.
I am the Light that lights the Way.

So let it be.

W.M.A

Keep Looking Up, My Friend

The thing about choosing to walk the Path of Ascension is this: you can no longer afford to habitually look down. You cannot indulge in the gravitational pull of endless drama, fear cycles, or the illusions parading as truth in the outer world. To ascend is to attune to higher frequency reception—vertically sourced, horizontally radiated. You receive from above to transmit outward, not the other way around. This is the rhythm of the Path.

To walk the Path of Light is to embody its vibration quietly, invisibly, and without seeking acknowledgment. That embodiment alone alters the field. Your silent presence—refined and luminous—creates transformation without effort. Words become secondary. Recognition may still come, for Light magnetizes attention, but the true initiate learns to hold that gaze with humility, not hunger. As your auric field becomes empowered, others will feel the shift. Some will be drawn in; others may recoil. Either way, you are fulfilling your role. The path will often lead to isolation—not as punishment, but as preparation.

When alone, reflect not only on what has been lost, but on what has been refined. Life is a matrix of interconnected events, sacred pressures pressing upon the psyche to refine perception. Ask: What energies now appear as obstacles, and how can I respond in a way that nourishes my Soul rather than my wounds? This simple shift in perspective is the beginning of transmutation. Victimhood solidifies the lower self; right response alchemizes it into Light.

Anchor yourself in a strong foundation of inner Self. From this root, all true manifestation unfolds. Home is not a building, but a vibration. It is the resonance of safety in one's own presence. That is sanctuary. And in that sanctuary, Divine Catharsis may erupt. These sacred eruptions—when energy clears and consciousness floods —are often misunderstood. Society may pathologize them, yet they are part of the transmutation process. I do not deny the need for careful integration, grounding, and wise counsel. But I do question the dominant psychiatric frameworks that view all non-ordinary states as delusion, rather than as calls from the Soul.

Wherever separation exists, error follows. That is the core simplicity of what the ancient texts call "sin." Disconnection from Source. Fragmentation from wholeness. And as terrifying as it may seem to confront this truth, it is liberating—because it can be healed. The return to Unity is not only possible—it is the Divine Plan itself. And as the Light of Pure Reason begins to dawn within the mind, one sees that the so-called "sins" of the world are simply distortions of consciousness. Realization becomes creative fire. Evolution becomes inevitable.

Consider how powerful just one of your thoughts is— when aligned. How transformative. The very awareness of this becomes a turning point. Yes, responsibility increases with awareness. But so does joy. So does liberation. When your thoughts become consecrated, when your heart aligns with the Soul, the world around you begins to reorganize. This is the sacred magnetism of right alignment.

It is through the sanctified temple of your own inner life—refined through meditation, discipline, and perseverance —that you enter the Ashrams of the Masters. You meet the Teacher not in the clouds, but in the fire of your own purified heart. The Dweller on the Threshold—the shadow self—guards that doorway, and only what is Light can pass through. This is the sacred work. And it is you who are both guardian and key-holder.

Affirm to yourself the truth you often forget: I believe, and I know. I have Faith, and I have Devotion. I love, and I am worthy of love, purely because I Am. Whisper this upon waking, and before sleep. Let it sing in your mind like a holy refrain. Mantram and affirmation carry far more spiritual power than any headline or social feed. Make them your inner architecture.

Pop culture, as paradoxical as it may sound, is the bridge into the future. The archetypes born there are prototypes of human evolution. But remember: the Builders are not Messiahs. The Lightworkers of the world, members of the New Group of World Servers, are not here to be worshipped—they are emanations of something greater: the Light of the World Teacher, the Coming One, the Embodiment of Love beyond all form. Align with that Emanation, not the ego of any personality.

Initiation requires more than faith. It demands reason illumined by the heart. It requires you to walk into the Light of Pure Reason—to understand it, to carry it, and then to turn back, descending from the summit to offer that Light to those still climbing. This return is the most sacred act of service. And it is never easy. To taste bliss and then walk back into shadow, for the sake of another—this is the path of the true disciple.

To serve is to surrender. To offer your Self not in pieces, but as a unified field of intention and compassion. That surrender does not diminish you—it completes you. And in it, you discover the profound joy of giving. Of seeing another soul light up because of something you remembered to embody.

There is a quiet clarity that comes when you realize the tides have shifted. You move from despair into devotion, from doubt into direction. But that movement is not accidental. It must be cultivated. Through conscious meditation, occult training, and right application, one begins to direct consciousness—not merely receive it. And this is what safeguards the seeker from the dangers of misalignment.

I know those dangers intimately. I have burned in the fires of fanaticism. I have wandered too far into visions without anchors. I share this as both warning and invitation. Do not fear the fire—but do not forget to ground it. Seek guidance. Practice discipline. And remember: zeal without wisdom becomes blindness. Wisdom without love becomes pride. Balance is the mark of the Soul's presence.

When the storms rise, you have two choices: to flail, or to surrender to the greater rhythm. To give yourself to the current of the Soul, and allow its intelligence to guide you. The Will of the Soul is never at odds with the Will of Source. It is the very outflow of that Will, stepped down through Hierarchy, through the Masters, through the

Ashram of your destiny. Align with it, and you will be drawn upward—into union with your Solar Angel, into the flame of conscious transformation.

At that altitude, you begin to understand what it means to be human. To be incarnate. The potential of the body, the mind, the heart—all begin to reveal themselves. Supernormal powers are not unnatural—they are perfectly natural, just unfamiliar. Humanity stands now at the edge of revelation. The borderland of miraculous capacity. And those who dare to align will inherit a world newly born through their awakening.

We are on the cusp. The veils thin. The Soul speaks. The time is now.

W.M.A.

Occult Meditation, Soul Integration & the White Magic Path

I want to bring your attention, emphatically, to the quiet miracle that begins to unfold in one's cognition as they deepen into a rhythm of occult meditation. Subtle at first —then undeniable—something begins to shift. Thought becomes clearer, not only in logic but in resonance. What once worked against you begins to serve you. Patterns invert, resistance fades, and synchronicities multiply. This is the fruit of gentle, loving awareness—not wishful thinking, but soul alignment. When you cease to chase desire and instead center yourself in the Will of the Creator, you discover the hidden truth: your deepest heart's longing was always part of the Plan.

In this state of alignment, events begin to reorganize themselves around your stillness. Life unfolds with a strange grace. Not always easy—but undeniably intelligent. You'll begin to witness how even adversity sharpens the diamond of your Soul. When faced with obstacles, those walking the Path learn to ask: What is this experience offering me in terms of mastery, alignment, and purification? Faith, rightly applied, is not naïve. It is an alchemical power.

Even the forces that appear to work against the Light are in fact contained within the Plan. The existence of the Dark Brotherhood—the oppositional force—is not a flaw but a necessity, for it fuels the evolution of contrast. The Light grows stronger in response. The Logos contains all things—not just joy, but tension; not just order, but the chaos that births it. Nothing is outside the scope of Divine Creation.

Blessings upon you.
Blessings within you.
Blessings without you.
Blessings rise like dew across your field in the Light of Pure Reason.

This life—fleeting and sacred—is but a drop in the infinite sea of your eternal becoming. In that light, what is an obstacle? What truly blocks the eternal? The statement, "If the Lord is behind you, none may stand against you," is not merely devotional—it is occult. It affirms that when one aligns with higher Will and embodies dispassionate wisdom, no obstruction can endure. The Soul knows its purpose. The personality must surrender.

The teachings of the Tibetan—channeled through Alice A. Bailey—make it clear that the Path of Detachment and Integration is the only true way forward. The mind must be trained to recognize illusion, the emotions brought into rhythm, and the body consecrated to Purpose. Through the Ageless Wisdom, one finds not dogma but Law— Living, Fire-born Truth that breathes through every tradition and speaks the same sacred directive: Know Thyself. Serve the Whole.

And in this knowing, even the simplest experiences become revelatory. The entire architecture of the Universe can be glimpsed in a single flower. A humble blade of grass is encoded with the same Divine Intelligence that births galaxies. This is not metaphor—it is occult fact. The vegetable kingdom speaks in silence, in pattern, in unfolding spirals of beauty. It reflects the order of the Logos. We have, for too long, separated ourselves from this conversation. But the Earth still whispers to those who listen.

You have likely been drawn to places of deep peace— energy vortexes, ancient groves, remote stones in the Earth's magnetic field. These are not romantic fantasies. They are sacred sites protected by the Building Devas and aligned to cosmic circuits. At such places, the human spirit can more easily receive its instructions. They are not required for contact—but they help. Wherever you are, you are of value. The poorest man may carry more spiritual authority than the priest. The hidden disciple may be more luminous than the teacher. Rank in Hierarchy is measured by Light, not labels.

Hierarchy is not a theory—it is a living force, now externalizing onto this Earth. For over a century, its subtle waves have been preparing the field. The false hierarchies —those based on wealth, status, and ego—are disintegrating. A new order of values is rising. Achievement will no longer be measured by material gain but by service, integrity, and radiatory influence. And what is rightfully yours, if it aligns with Purpose, is already moving toward you.

So do not cling to anxious anticipation. Expectancy is good. Obsession is not. The enemy of expansion is the unrest of the personal mind. Often, it is our own personality that manifests as our oppressor—generating anxiety, despair, and exhaustion. But once you root yourself in the Infinite, something begins to shift. When you realize your Soul has no endpoint, how can you fear loss? When you remember you are eternal, how can you be enslaved by time?

This realization changes everything. True individuality is not erased in the Group Soul—it is magnified. You become more distinctly yourself as you harmonize with the Whole. Integration does not dissolve identity—it reveals its divine tone. And in that realization comes ecstatic joy. Not happiness, but freedom. A release of psychic pressure. The remembrance that your consciousness does not, and cannot, end.

"It is through dying that one awakens to eternal life."
This occult truth, spoken by the Christ, is not about physical death. It is about the death of illusion—the fading of the personal self and the shattering of the causal body. This is Soul Integration. The Light body is not fantasy. It is the logical conclusion of a system composed of vibrating particles and electric atoms. Transfiguration begins with consciousness, but it extends to matter. The higher vibrates through the lower until the lower is transformed.

"I am the Light of the World," said the Christ—and so too will you be, when the Soul fully anchors in form. This is not egoic declaration, but sacred law. The one who has realized Light becomes Light. The one who walks the Way becomes the Way. And that Way is paved by right motive, pure heart, and unwavering devotion to the Plan.

True White Magic is the application of Will in alignment with Love for the sake of Service. No selfish endeavor can taint it. A Treatise on White Magic, given through A.A.B., lays down clear rules—not as limitations, but as protective scaffolding. These rules are veiled intentionally. They are difficult by design. Only those willing to meditate, to ponder, and to strive will discover the truths embedded within. But once discovered, they become keys.

Approach this Work with humility, and never alone. Seek guidance. Study deeply. For to misunderstand White Magic is to risk stepping into grey or even black magic—often without knowing. The dangers are real. The toll can be high. Psychic damage, emotional imbalance, even physical harm can result from misapplication. And these effects do not end with you. Magic touches the field, and the field includes others. The Law is not sentimental. It is exact.

Those of us in the New Group of World Servers are generally protected by our alignment, but that does not absolve us of responsibility. We are guardians—not only of Light, but of humanity itself. And we do not tolerate the deliberate use of occult force for personal gain. The Will of the Soul is to serve. White Magic exists only for the Plan and the elevation of all beings.

A final word for those on the path: You may at times desire to gently disturb those around you—not with cruelty, but with authenticity. This is right. The Light disturbs. The truth unsettles. It triggers. And that is part of the Work. Live unapologetically. The effect of a soul-aligned life is often disruptive to personalities still ruled by fear. But do not shrink. Your presence alone can alter someone's trajectory.

If you are misunderstood—so be it. If you are attacked—remember, their time is ending. The world of falsehood is collapsing. Its institutions, though loud and desperate, are dying. Like a wounded beast, they will lash out before falling. But fall they must.

You were born for this hour.

Do not let the old world trick you into fear. Do not question, even for a moment, the inevitability of Hierarchy's return and the triumph of Light. There is no shadow that Light cannot penetrate. There is no harm that cannot be transmuted by the energies now streaming from Shamballa, flowing through Hierarchy, and into the receptive hearts of humanity.

Above all else, trust.
Trust the higher order.
Trust the Love that fuels it.

Love is synonymous with Pure Reason. It is intelligent, coordinated, and purposeful. Those who serve the Plan are known by their actions, not their claims. Watch those in power—not as a partisan, but as a soul. Look through the eyes of synthesis. Do they build or destroy? Do they unify or divide?

This discernment is sacred. Use it wisely. Use it as a servant of the Light.

W.M.A.

A Treatise on Cosmic Fire
Continuation of Excerpt from A.A.B.

As time proceeds, man will gradually do four things:

1. Recover past knowledge and powers developed in Atlantean days.
2. Produce bodies resistant to the fire elementals of the lower kind which work in the mineral kingdom.
3. Comprehend the inner meaning of radioactivity, or the setting loose of the power inherent in all elements and all atoms of chemistry, and in all true minerals.
4. Reduce the formulas of the coming chemists and scientists to *SOUND*, and not simply formulate through experiment to pater. In this last statement lies (for those who can perceive) the most illuminating hint that it has been possible as yet to impart on this matter.

It may seem that I have not communicated much information anent this conscious manipulation of the fires. That lies in the inability of the student to read the esoteric background of the above communicated statements. Conscious transmutation is possible only when a man has transmuted the elements in his own vehicles; then only can he be trusted with the secrets of divine alchemy.

When through the latent internal fires of the matter of his own sheaths he has transmuted the chemical and mineral atoms of those sheaths, then can he safely —through affinity of substance—aid the work of mineral transmutation of the first has transmuted the correspondence to the vegetable kingdom within his own organism can he chemically do work of the of the second order. Only when the fires of mind in himself dominate, can he work with the transmutative processes of the third order, or with the transference of life into the animal forms. Only when the Self within, or the Ego in the causal body, is in control of has threefold personality can he occultly be permitted to be an alchemist of the fourth order, and work in connection with the transmutation of the animal monad into the human kingdom, with all the vast knowledge that is included in that idea. Much lies ahead to be accomplished, but the appreciation of the magnitude of the task need be no place for discouragement, for in the wise outlining of the future, in the cautious promulgation of knowledge concerning the necessitated stages, will come strenuous effort and aim on the part of many aspirants, and the evolutionary bringing in of those who can achieve.

The problem of speaking clearly on this subject of transmutation is a very real one, owing to the vastness of the subject and the fact that in the transmutation process the magician or alchemist *works with deva essence through the control of the lesser Builders in cooperation with the greater Devas*. In order, therefore, to bring about clarity of thought and definiteness of conjecture in this respect, I desire primarily to lay down certain postulates, which must be carefully borne in mind when considering this question of transmutation. They are five in number and concern specifically the field wherein the transmuting process is carried on. The student must recollect at this juncture the distinction that made between the work of the black and the white magician. It might be helpful here before proceeding further to look at these distinctions as far as they concern the matter in hand:

First. The light Brother deals with positive electrical energy. The dark Brother deals with the negative electrical energy.

Second. The white Magician occupies himself with the soul of things. The black Magician centers his attention upon the form.

Third. The white Magician develops the inherent energy of the sphere concerned (whether human, animal, vegetable, or mineral) and produces results through the self-induced activities of the central life, subhuman, human, or super-human. The black Magician attains results through the agency of force external to the sphere involved, and produces transmutation through the agency of resolvents (if so I might term it) or through the method of the reduction of the form, rather than through radiation, as does the white Magician.

These differences of method need to be carefully considered and their reaction visualized in connection with different elements, atoms, and forms. To return to our statement of our five postulates anent the transmutation of substance, the resolution of the life, or the transference of energy into different forms.

The Five Postulates of Transmutation

Postulate I. All matter is living matter, or is the vital substance of deva entities. For instance, a plane, and forms built of that particular plan substance, is the material form sheath of a great Deva, who is the essence back of manifestation and the soul of the plane.

Postulate II. All forms, vibrating to any keynote, are fabricated by the building devas out of the matter of their own bodies. Hence they are called the great Mother aspect, for they produce the form out of their own substance.

Postulate III. The devas are the life which produces form-cohesion. They are the third and second aspects, blended, and might be considered as the life of all forms that are subhuman. A magician, therefore, who transmutes in the mineral kingdom works practically with the deva essence in its earliest form on the upward arc of evolution, and has to remember three things:

    a. The effect of the backward pull of the involutionary lives which lie back of the mineral or, in effect, its heredity.

    b. The sevenfold nature of the peculiar group of devas which constitute its *being* in an occult sense.

    c. The next transition stage ahead into the vegetable kingdom, or the occult effect of the second kingdom on the first.

Postulate IV. All deva essences and builders on the physical plane are peculiarly dangerous to man, for they work on the etheric levels and are— as I have earlier pointed out—the transmitters of prana, or the vital, animating substance, and hence they set loose upon the ignorant and the unwary, fiery essence which burns and destroys.

Postulate V. The devas do not work as individualized conscious units through self-initiating purposes as does a man, a Heavenly Man or a solar Logos (viewed as Egos) but they work in groups subject to:

 a. Inherent impulse, or latent active intelligence.
 b. Orders issued by the greater Builders.
 c. Ritual, or compulsion induced though color and sound.

When these facts are remembered and considered, some comprehension of the place the devas play in transmutation may be achieved. The position that the fire occupies in the process is of peculiar interest here, for it brings out clearly the difference of method between the two schools.

In the transmutative process as carried on by the Brotherhood, the inner fire which animates the atom, form or man is stimulated, fanned and strengthened till it (through its own internal potency) burns up its sheaths, and escapes by radiation from within its ring-pass-not. This is seen in an interesting way as occurring during the process of the final initiation when the causal body is destroyed by fire. The fire within burns up all else and the electric fire escapes. The true alchemist therefore in days to come will in every case seek to stimulate the radioactivity of the element or atom with which he is working and will center his attention upon the *positive* nucleus. By increasing its vibration, its activity, or its positivity, he will bring about the desired end. The Masters do this in connection with the human spirit and do not concern Themselves at all with this 'deva' aspect. The same basic rule will be found to apply in the case of a mineral as well as of a man.

The process as carried on by the Dark Brotherhood is the reverse of this. They center the attention upon the form, and seek to shatter and break that form, or the combination of atoms, in order to permit the central electric life to escape. They bring about this result through external agencies and by availing themselves of the destructive nature of the substance (deva essence) itself. They burn and destroy the material sheath, seeking to imprison the escaping volatile essence as the form disintegrates.

This hinders the evolutionary plan in the case of the life involved, delays the consummation, interferes with the ordered progress of development, and puts all the factors involved in a bad position. The life (or entity) concerned receives a setback, the devas work destructively, and without participation in the purpose of the plan, and the magician is in danger, under the Law of Karma, and through the materializing of his own substance by affinity with the third aspect. Black magic of this nature creeps into all religions along this very line of destruction of the form through outer agency, and not through the liberation of the life through inner development and preparedness. It produces the evils of Hatha Yoga in India and similar methods as practiced in certain religious and occult orders in the Occident also. Both work with matter on some plane in the three worlds, and do evil that good may come; both control the devas, and attempt to produce specific ends by manipulation of the matter of the form. The Hierarchy works with the soul within the form and produces results that are intelligent, self-induced, and permanent. Wherever attention is centered on the form and not on the Spirit, the tendency is to deva worship, deva contact, and black magic, for the *form* is made of deva substance on all planes.

This must be considered well in connection with every form for it holds the key to many mysteries.

THE PARTICIPANTS IN THE MYSTERIES

The participants in the mysteries are generally known, and no secret has been made of the general personnel and procedure.   It is only sought here to impart a greater sense of reality to the data already given by a fuller exposition and a more pointed reference to the parts played by such during the ceremony.   At this stage the student would be wise to bear in mind certain things as he ponders upon the mysteries touched upon here:—

That care must be taken to interpret all here given in terms of spirit and not of matter or form.   We are dealing entirely with the subjective or consciousness aspect of manifestation, and with that which lies back of the objective form. This realization will save the student from much later confusion.

That we are considering facts which are substantial and real on the *mental plane*—the plane on which all the major initiations take place—but which are not materialized on the physical plane, and are not physical plane phenomena. The link between the two planes exists in the continuity of consciousness which the initiate will have developed, and which will enable him to bring through to the physical brain, occurrences and happenings upon the subjective planes of life.

CORROBORATION OF INITIATION

Corroboration of these occurrences, and proof of the accuracy of the transmitted knowledge will demonstrate as follows:—

In and through the etheric centers. These centers will be greatly stimulated, and will, through their increased inherent energy, enable the initiate to accomplish more in the path of service than he ever before dreamed possible. His dreams and ideals become, not possibilities, but demonstrating facts in manifestation.

The physical center, such as the pineal gland and the pituitary body, will begin to develop rapidly, and he will become conscious of the awakening of the "siddhis," or powers of the soul, in the higher connotation of the words. He will be aware of the process of conscious control, and of the self-initiated manipulations of the above powers. He will realize the methods of egoic contact and the right direction of force.

The nervous system, through which the emotional body or astral nature works, will become highly sensitized, yet strong withal. The brain will become ever more rapidly an acute transmitter of the inner impulses. This fact is of real importance, and will bring about—as its significance becomes more apparent—a revolution in the attitude of educators, of physicians and others, to the development of the nervous system and the healing of nervous disorders.

Occult memory.   The initiate finally becomes aware increasingly of the growth of that inner recollection, or "occult memory," which concerns the work of the Hierarchy and primarily his share in the general plan. When the initiate, who occultly recalls, in his waking consciousness, a ceremonial fact, finds all these manifestations of increased growth and conscious realization *in himself*, then the truth of his inner assurance is proven and substantiated to him.

It must be remembered that this inner substantiation is of no value to anyone but the initiate.   He has to prove himself to the outer world through his life of service and the work accomplished and thereby call forth from all his environing associates a recognition that will show itself in a sanctified emulation and a strenuous effort to tread the same path, actuated ever by the same motive,—that of service and brotherhood, not self-aggrandizement and selfish acquirement.   It should also be remembered that if the above is true in connection with the work, it is still more true in connection with the initiate himself. *Initiation is a strictly personal matter with a universal application.*   It rests upon his inner attainment.   The initiate will know for himself when the event occurs and needs no one to tell him of it.   The expansion of consciousness called initiation must include the physical brain or it is of no value.   As those lesser expansions of consciousness which we undergo normally every day, and call "learning" something or other, have reference to the apprehension by the physical brain of an imparted fact or apprehended circumstance, so with the greater expansions which are the outcome of the many lesser.

At the same time, it is quite possible for men to be functioning on the physical plane and to be actively employed in world service who have no recollection of having undergone the initiatory process, yet who, nevertheless, may have taken the first or second initiation in a previous or earlier life. This is the result, simply, of a lack of "bridging" from one life to another, or it may be the outcome of a definite decision by the Ego. A man may be able better to work off certain karma and to carry out certain work for the Lodge if he is free from occult occupation and mystic introspection during the period of any one earth life. There are many such amongst the sons of men at this time who have previously taken the first initiation, and a few who have taken the second, but who are nevertheless quite unaware of it, yet their centers and nervous organization carry proof to those who have the inner vision. If initiation is taken for the first time in any life, the recollection of it extends to the physical brain.

Curiosity, or even ordinary good living, never brought a man to the Portal of Initiation. Curiosity, by arousing a strong vibration in a man's lower nature, only serves to swing him away from, instead of towards the goal he is interested in; whilst ordinary good living, when not furthered by a life of utter sacrifice for others, and by a reticence, humility, and disinterestedness of a very unusual kind, may serve to build good vehicles which will be of use in another incarnation, but will not serve to break down those barriers, outer and inner, and overcome those opposing forces and energies which stand between a "good" man and the ceremony of initiation.

The Path of Discipleship is a difficult one to tread, and the Path of Initiation harder still; an initiate is but a battle-scarred warrior, the victor in many a hard-won fight; he speaks not of his achievements, for he is too busy with the great work in hand; he makes no reference to himself or to all that he has accomplished, save to deprecate the littleness of what has been done. Nevertheless, to the world he is ever a man of large influence, the wielder of spiritual power, the embodier of ideals, the worker for humanity, who unfailingly brings results which succeeding generations will recognize. He is one who, in spite of all this great achievement, is seldom understood by his own generation. He is frequently the butt of men's tongues, and frequently all that he does is misinterpreted; he lays his all—time, money, influence, reputation, and all that the world considers worth while—upon the altar of altruistic service, and frequently offers his life as a final gift, only to find that those whom he has served throw his gift back to him, scorn his renunciation, and label him with unsavory names. But the initiate cares not, for his is the privilege to see somewhat into the future, and therefore he realizes that the force he has generated will in due course of time bring to fulfillment the plan; he knows also that his name and effort are noted in the archives of the Lodge, and that the "Silent Watcher" over the affairs of men has taken notice.

PLANETARY EXISTENCES.

In considering now the personalities taking part in the initiation ceremonies, the first to be dealt with are Those Who are termed Planetary Existences. This refers to those great Beings who, for a period of planetary manifestation, overshadow or stay with our humanity. They are not very many in number, for the majority of the Great Ones pass on steadily and increasingly to other and higher work, as Their places can be taken and Their functions carried on by members of our earth evolution, both deva and human.

Among Those directly connected with our Lodge of Masters in its various divisions upon the planet, the following might be enumerated:-

The "*Silent Watcher*," that great Entity Who is the informing life of the planet, and Who holds the same position to the Lord of the World, Sanat Kumara, as the Ego does to the lower self of man. Some idea of the high stage of evolution of this Great Being may be gathered from the analogous degree of evolutionary difference existing between a human being and a perfected adept. From the standpoint of our planetary scheme, this Great Life has no greater, and He is, as far as we are concerned, a correspondence to the personal God of the Christian. He works through His representative on the physical plane, Sanat Kumara, Who is the focal point for His life and energy. He holds the world within His aura. This great Existence is only contacted directly by the adept who has taken the fifth initiation, and is proceeding to take the other two, the sixth and seventh. Once a year, at the Wesak Festival, the Lord Buddha, sanctioned by the Lord of the World, carries to the assembled humanity a dual stream of force, that emanating from the Silent Watcher, supplemented by the more focalized energy of the Lord of the World. This dual energy He pours out in blessing over the people gathered at the ceremony in the Himalayas, and from them in turn it flows out to all peoples and tongues and races. It may not perhaps be generally known that at a certain crisis during the Great War [WW I], the Hierarchy of our planet deemed it well nigh necessary to invoke the aid of the Silent Watcher, and —employing the great mantram whereby the Buddha can be reached—called the attention of the latter, and sought his agency with the Planetary Logos. In consultation between the Planetary Logos, the Lord of the World, one of the Buddhas of Activity, the Buddha, the Mahachohan, and the Manu (these names are given in order of their relative evolutionary stage) it was decided to watch proceedings a little longer before interfering with the trend of affairs, as the karma of the planet would have been delayed should the strife have been ended too soon. Their confidence in the ability of men duly to adjust conditions was justified, and interference proved needless. This conference took place at Shamballa. This is mentioned to show the close scrutiny given to everything concerning the affairs of men by the various Planetary Existences. It is literally true, in an occult sense, that "not a sparrow falleth" without its fall being noticed.

It may be asked why the Bodhisattva was not included in the conference. The reason was that the war was in the department of the Manu, and members of the Hierarchy concern Themselves with that which is strictly Their own business; the Mahachohan, being the embodiment of the intelligent or manasic principle, participates in all conferences. In the next great strife the department of religions will be involved, and the Bodhisattva intimately concerned. His Brother, the Manu, will then be relatively exempt, and will proceed with His own affairs. And yet withal there is the closest co-operation in all departments, with no loss of energy. Owing to the unity of consciousness of those who are free from the three lower planes, what transpires in one department is known in the others

As the Planetary Logos is only concerned in the two final initiations, which are not compulsory as are the earlier five, it serves no purpose to enlarge upon His work. These initiations are taken upon the buddhic and atmic planes, whereas the first five are taken upon the mental.

The Lord of the World, the One Initiator, He Who is called in the Bible "The Ancient of Days," and in the Hindu Scriptures the First Kumara, He, Sanat Kumara it is, Who from His throne at Shamballa in the Gobi desert, presides over the Lodge of Masters, and holds in His hands the reins of government in all the three departments. Called in some Scriptures "the Great Sacrifice," He has chosen to watch over the evolution of men and devas until all have been occultly "saved." He it is Who decides upon the "advancements" in the different departments, and Who settles who shall fill the vacant posts; He it is Who, four times a year, meets in conference with all the Chohans and Masters, and authorizes what shall be done to further the ends of evolution.

Occasionally, too, He meets with initiates of lesser degree, but only at times of great crises, when some individual is given the opportunity to bring peace out of strife, and to kindle a blaze whereby rapidly crystallizing forms are destroyed and the imprisoned life consequently set free.

At stated periods in the year the Lodge meets, and at the Wesak Festival gathers under His jurisdiction for three purposes:

1. To contact planetary force through the medium of the Buddha.

2. To hold the principal of the quarterly conferences.

3. To admit to the ceremony of initiation those who are ready in all grades.

Three other initiation ceremonies take place during the year:—

1. For the minor initiations administered by the Bodhisattva, all of which are in the department of the

Mahachohan, and on one or other of the four lesser rays, the rays of attribute.

2. For the major initiations on one or other of the three major rays, the rays of aspect, which are administered by the Bodhisattva, and are therefore the first two initiations.

3. For the higher three initiations at which Sanat Kumara wields the Rod.

At all initiations the Lord of the World is present, but at the first two He holds a position similar to that held by the Silent Watcher, when Sanat Kumara administers the oath at the third, fourth and fifth initiations.   His power streams forth and the flashing forth of the star before the initiate is the signal of His approval, but the initiate does not see Him face to face until the third initiation.

The function of the *three Kumaras*, or the three Buddhas of Activity at initiation is interesting.   They are three aspects of the one aspect, and the pupils of Sanat Kumara.   Though Their functions are many and varied, and concern primarily the forces and energies of nature, and the direction of the building agencies, They have a vital connection with the applicant for initiation, inasmuch as They each embody the force or energy of one or other of the three higher sub-planes of the mental plane.   Therefore at the third initiation one of these Kumaras transmits to the causal body of the initiate that energy which destroys third sub-plane matter, and thus brings about part of the destruction of the vehicle; at the fourth initiation another Buddha transmits second plane force, and at the fifth, first sub-plane force is similarly passed into the remaining atoms of the causal vehicle, producing the final liberation. The work done by the second Kumara, with second sub-plane force, is in this solar system the most important in connection with the egoic body, and produces its complete dissipation, whereas the final application causes the atoms themselves (which formed that body) to disperse.

During the initiation ceremony, when the initiate stands before the Lord of the World, these three great Beings form a triangle, within whose lines of force the initiate finds himself. At the first two initiations, wherein the Bodhisattva functions as the Hierophant, the Mahachohan, the Manu, and a Chohan who temporarily represents the second department perform a similar office. At the highest two initiations, those three Kumaras who are called "the esoteric Kumaras" form a triangle wherein the initiate stands, when he faces the Planetary Logos.

These facts are imparted to teach two things, first, the unity of the method, second, that the truism "as above so below" is an occult fact in nature.

At the final two initiations many members of the Hierarchy who are, if one might so express it, extra-planetary, and who function outside the dense physical and the etheric globe of our planet, take part, but a stricter enumeration is needless. Sanat Kumara is still the Hierophant, yet in a very esoteric manner it is the Planetary Logos Himself who officiates. They are merged at that time into one Identity, manifesting different aspects.

Suffice it to say, in concluding this brief statement, that the making of an initiate is an affair with a dual effect, for it involves ever a passing on of some adept or initiate to a higher grade or to other work, and the coming in under the Law of some human being who is in process of attainment. Therefore it is a thing of great moment, involving group activity, group loyalty, and united endeavour, and much may depend upon the wisdom of admitting a man to high office and to a place in the council chambers of the Hierarchy.

A Treatise on Cosmic Fire
A.A.B.

Daily Visualizations for the Stages of the Great Work

To internalize the sacred alchemy of the Soul, seekers may engage with the following visualizations, one for each stage of the Great Work. These practices offer a meditative anchor to align inner life with the rhythm of spiritual transmutation. Alongside each stage is an indication of the inner signs that suggest readiness to proceed, with the understanding that individual timelines vary. This is a process of attunement rather than achievement.

1. Nigredo – The Blackening
Approximate Duration: 1–6 months (or more)
Visualization: Sit in stillness. Visualize yourself descending into a dark cavern deep beneath the earth. You are alone in sacred silence, surrounded by black stone. Feel every thought, habit, and false identity fall away. You are raw, stripped of pretense. Accept the discomfort. See a single coal glowing faintly before you—this is the unformed light of your truth. Sit with it.

Signs of Readiness to Move Forward:

- You've stopped resisting emotional darkness.

- Self-awareness is increasing.

- Old patterns are breaking down, willingly or through external challenge.

2. Albedo – The Whitening
Approximate Duration: 2–8 months
Visualization: Visualize a soft, silver-white mist pouring

into the cave. It begins to cleanse the walls, the coal, your body. It softens your grief, pain, and regrets. See this mist lift the coal gently until it levitates, glowing softly. Begin to feel peace. The past is forgiven. You begin to remember who you truly are.

Signs of Readiness to Move Forward:

- Increased clarity and emotional neutrality.

- You begin to intuit subtle truths.

- The impulse to serve others awakens.

3. Citrinitas – The Yellowing

Approximate Duration: 3–12 months

Visualization: From the white mist, golden light now begins to radiate outward. The cavern fades, and you are standing in a field at dawn. The sky is lit by a golden sun rising in the east. Visualize the golden light streaming into your mind, activating wisdom. Symbols appear before you —teachings, inner revelations. Receive them with joy.

Signs of Readiness to Move Forward:

- You feel inspired by study, symbolism, and teachings.

- Your intuition and logic now work together.

- You begin building structures in your life that reflect your inner clarity.

4. Rubedo – The Reddening

Approximate Duration: 1–2 years or longer
Visualization: See the golden light intensify into ruby fire. The sun is now at its zenith, and its rays ignite your body into radiant light. You are no longer in a cave or a field— you are the flame itself. Feel your aura vibrate with spiritual will and loving purpose. See your Soul radiating outward, forming bridges to others, creating and healing.

Signs of Completion:

- The will to serve is consistent and joyful.

- Your life expresses your inner truth.

- You experience glimpses of divine unity through daily life.

The true alchemist is one who transmutes suffering into service, illusion into illumination. You are not meant to rush these stages, but to become them. Through daily contact with the light of your Soul, the Great Work ceases to be a process and becomes your very Being.

CHAPTER VII

THE LATENT POWERS OF THE SOUL

*"The Fire sleeps within the seed; awaken it, and the Soul
becomes the scribe of Heaven."*

The Path Transforms

I believe it is time to move forward onto a more potent and personal line of thought. The process of alignment was explored deeply in my previous text, *The Dawn Approaches: A New World Order*, and here, I write with the assumption that you, the reader, have not only encountered the occult approach—but practiced it. That you have begun to observe its results. Let us now enter into the latent powers of the Soul and their emergence through a causal body that has, hopefully, become more intact, vitalized, and directed.

This is the way of the true occultist and the beginning of the path of the Agni Yogi—the one who no longer "practices magic" in the traditional sense, but who co-creates reality through the Fire of the Mind. We'll explore that sacred path in greater depth shortly, but before we reach that point, a distinction must be made between White Magic as a system of spiritual science and the yogic fire-path of inner transmutation that transcends all forms.

The first and most vital truth to affirm is this: without the active practice of Perfect Harmlessness, no work can remain white. One's efforts, if even subtly tinged with self-seeking, begin to shift toward grey, and if left unchecked, may fall in resonance with the work of the Dark Brotherhood—whether intentionally or unconsciously. I know this from experience. In my own missteps, I have witnessed the splintering of energy that occurs when selfish intent is masked beneath spiritual ambition. The repair of those spiritual fractures is not a small task. It often requires assistance from a teacher or presence further along the Path. It is always humbling.

Let me share a truth from my own past. As a child, I was magnetically drawn to all things mystical—rituals, orders, theories, spells. I wasn't searching for power so much as for proof. Proof that Magic was real, that the otherworldly things I sensed and remembered had a foundation. As I grew older, I began to imitate what I read and consumed. I copied what I saw. I repeated words I didn't yet understand. And because I was earnest, the forces I invited responded in full.

It wasn't until after my eighteenth year that the effects became severe. They weren't just "spiritual symptoms"— they were supernormal phenomena, psychological disturbances, and deeply destabilizing internal shifts. What I didn't know then was this: the Fire of the Soul, when contacted prematurely or ungrounded, can become the Fire of Madness. The Great Equalizer applies pressure to the entire system. If that system is fractured, unbalanced, or filled with unintegrated shadow, the fire does not heal—it burns. It tears through the body, through relationships, through the delicate cords of mental order.

This is not a metaphor. This is an occult law.

For some, the karmic burden of misused power carries across lifetimes. For others, it seduces them into trying to manipulate the very fire that is destroying them. This is the trap of black magic: the desperate desire to control what is asking you to surrender. The fire does not yield to will—it yields to alignment.

When I reached young adulthood, I found what I thought was freedom—but it was a descent into preparation. My vow was clear: No matter the cost, I would know the Truth. I would walk the path of awakening—even if it undid me. And it did.

From that moment on, everything I had summoned—every spell, every word, every karmic imprint from past lives and ancestral work—rose up. Not to punish me, but to demand integration. And as I began to touch the Light I had longed for, I found myself in a paradox—experiencing the highest states of ecstatic insight and simultaneously enduring the greatest threats to my sanity, safety, and soul. It felt like two lives, two timelines, running concurrently and burning against each other. And through that tension, I was reshaped.

There are people—strangers even—whose lives I impacted just by walking near them, whose fields responded to the energy pouring off my unstable magnetic body. Some of them may never know. Some of them do. This is the truth about power: you cannot separate intention from impact. Even the desire to help, if projected without invitation, can become a subtle violation. The only exception to this law of non-interference comes from Hierarchy itself, and even then, the sacredness of free will is never breached.

What brought me back? What aligned me again?

Relentless aspiration to the Truth. Through every Dark Night, I never let go of the reality of the higher realms. Once the fire has touched your Spirit and lit your mind, the world cannot satisfy you. The Soul leaves a scent behind, and it will call you home.

I write this now as both a warning and a blessing: you can avoid much of the suffering I endured. Recognize the dangers of glamour. Do not attempt to take the fire. Prepare yourself to receive it. Look inward—not only to see where you still act from separation, but to begin building your shield of harmlessness, forged from love, humility, and precision. The Masters, especially Morya, have spoken clearly: when the intention is righteous, the Disciple shall be shielded by the radiance of Hierarchy. But no one—not even a Master—can override the Law of Free Will. It is up to you.

We lost much potential in the old cycle. So many Souls called, so few fully prepared. But in this new chapter, under the seed vibration of the New World Order—the true spiritual Order of alignment and synthesis—schools will rise. Initiates will gather. And the scientific method of spiritual alignment will be taught openly once more. Under Capricorn's guidance and Aquarius' flow, this generation will build the bridge that others may walk.

Celebrate the New Year in Aries, dear one. Align your personal cycles to the rhythm of the heavens. The warrior in you is needed.

———

In this space—between breaths, between the flicker of thoughts—I find my peace. I've always been sensitive to the chaotic energies of others, and for most of my life, their thoughts swirled through my own mind like storm winds. But now, with Hierarchy and my Teacher walking beside me, I am anchored. I can feel my center. The Will within me is clear. Directed. Unshakable.

I was born to write. Not for fame, but for Function.

Even as a child, I would draw symbols from languages I hadn't learned, invent alphabets that seemed to echo something ancient. Only now do I recognize these marks as remnants—Atlantean echoes from past lives. But I no longer chase the past. I understand the danger in becoming obsessed with what was. That is not our path. Ours is the Way Forward.

The blessing of Infinity lies ahead. We stand now in the present, shaping the form of the future with every act, every breath, every conscious choice. Some of us may be nearing our final incarnations in this cycle. Others may return again, but not in forgetfulness. The Day is coming when the veil will not drop again.

The Group Soul does not devour your individuality—it amplifies it. The personality may fear losing itself, but what actually dissolves is the mask, the illusion of separation. When we enter the larger field of spiritual Brotherhood, we do not become less—we become more truly ourselves.

Was not Christ Himself a radiant individual?

And yet—He was the Way, not because of exclusivity, but because He became a living example of what is possible for all. Through the disciplines of countless incarnations, the World Teacher refined His vessel to such a point that it could hold the full Light of Godhead. This is the path. His path is not separate from ours. He waits for us still.

W.M.A.

Take a breath with me now. A sacred pause.
Breathe in... four counts...
Hold... four counts...
Exhale... four counts...
Hold... four counts...
And again...

You are here. You are ready.
The Work is waiting.
Let us walk the fire—together.

The Path of the Agni Yogi

There comes a point in the Work where the rituals fall away—not in rejection, but in transcendence. Not because they were wrong, but because their fire has already done its job. That fire lives inside now, not just in the candles, not just in the invocations. This is the beginning of the path of the Agni Yogi.

To walk the way of the Agni Yogi is to become a flame that no longer needs fuel. One steps into the silence not because they are empty, but because they are full. Thought becomes directive. Will becomes aligned. Magic becomes natural—not because it has ceased, but because it has become indistinguishable from presence itself.

The Agni Yogi does not practice magic in the old sense. They are the ritual. Their mind is not an instrument—they are the fire that directs it. Their body is not a vessel of burden—it is an altar. Their emotions are not distractions —they are smoke rising from a sacred hearth. This is the integration of the Triad. This is mind, heart, and will united in flame.

The path is not easy, nor is it meant to be. It is not a rejection of the world, but the fiercest embrace of it. Agni Yoga is not aesthetic—it is alchemical. The fire burns impurities on sight. It leaves nothing untouched, but what it reveals is what has always been eternal within you.

We will speak more on this—on the distinctions between White Magic and this higher path of co-creation through the Fire of Mind. We will map the disciplines, the dangers, and the divine rewards. But first, we must remember:

You do not call down this fire.
You become worthy of its descent.
And then, you tend it.

Practices and Disciplines of the Agni Yogi

The Agni Yogi does not follow a rigid outer structure. The discipline is not in performance, but in inner posture. What is required is not formality, but constancy. The Fire of Mind is not lit by repetition alone, but by precision, purity, and purpose. It responds to truth. It responds to presence. It responds to your ability to hold stillness while walking in the flame.

So what, then, is the daily path?

The first and most important discipline is inner alignment before outward action. No step is taken unless it flows from Soul recognition. The Agni Yogi rises not with an agenda, but with an invocation:

What is mine to do today, in service of the Plan?

This act of listening—truly listening—becomes a discipline unto itself. The Agni Yogi trains the inner ear, polishes the lens, and returns to the altar of silence until the Fire speaks.

Second is conscious thought-formation. The Agni Yogi does not waste thought. Thought is fire. Each idea is a spark that can either burn clean or burn blind. This path requires the practice of harmlessness in thought—not just toward others, but toward oneself. Every thought projected becomes a link in the chain of future manifestation. This is not a metaphor. It is law.

Third is will training. The Agni Yogi is not swayed by mood or impulse. They know that the personality will try to override the Soul. So they learn to pause. To delay reaction. To observe sensation without identifying with it. They train the will like one would train a blade—sharpened not by violence, but by precision. This is how one moves from occult student to conscious servant.

Fourth is purification through contact. Not all fire is ignited alone. The Agni Yogi learns to recognize those whose presence awakens their flame—and they seek to uplift others in kind. This discipline is not about surrounding oneself with "like-minded" people. It is about learning to see the flame in everyone, regardless of its brightness. Hierarchy works through relationship. And so must the Yogi.

Fifth is the practice of dispassionate service. This is not coldness—it is clarity. The Agni Yogi serves without attachment to results. Without pride. Without expectation of recognition. They are disciplined in letting go, even as they give everything. Service becomes not an obligation, but a sacrament. Each act is an offering. Each moment, an altar.

And finally, there is daily invocation of Fire—not through drama, but through sincerity. Whether it is through silent mantram, contemplative writing, soul-aligned movement, or sacred breath, the Agni Yogi feeds the inner flame daily. Not out of fear of its fading—but because the fire is alive, and it grows when honored.

There is no rulebook here. There are only laws. Laws of soul vibration. Laws of energy response. Laws of Light. And the Agni Yogi does not obey them out of fear, but out of love for the Fire itself.

These are not disciplines to bind the spirit. They are tools to *free* it.

And if practiced with humility, devotion, and exactitude— **they will make you a vessel fit for sacred fire.**

Ritual Magic vs. the Fire of Mind

Ritual magic is beautiful. Sacred. Powerful. It marks the beginning of conscious co-creation. It teaches the practitioner rhythm, intention, symbolic correspondence, and the sacred architecture of energy. It builds the habit of devotion. But the Agni Yogi stands beyond the temple— not in superiority, but in absorption.

Ritual calls down fire.

The Agni Yogi becomes it.

Ritual uses form to generate contact.

The Agni Yogi uses contact to dissolve form.

This is not to diminish the ritual path. Without ritual, most would never begin. But there comes a time when the tools must be set down. Not discarded—transcended. The wand, the circle, the candle, the altar—they are all outer reflections of inner forces. The Agni Yogi has no need to cast a circle because they themselves have become one.

The path of ritual magic is the path of symbolic invocation. The Fire of Mind is direct radiation. It does not require incantation or gesture—it requires alignment. The will must be fused with the Soul. The mind must be as still as a mountain lake. The heart must burn without smoke. Only then does the higher fire descend—not to perform, but to transform.

Ritual magic is ruled by timing—planetary hours, moon phases, sacred calendars. The Fire of Mind is timeless. It speaks in the present moment and bypasses the gates of astrological restriction. When you are in right alignment, you are always on time. The Logos is not bound by calendar.

Another key difference: ritual magic often seeks to influence. The Fire of Mind seeks to reveal. It is not about bending energy to will, but about dissolving all distortion so that Will flows through you without obstruction. This is what makes the Agni Yogi dangerous to the old world: they do not need permission to burn clean.

And where ritual magic builds connection with beings, symbols, and spirits—the Agni Yogi invokes only the Soul. The Soul is the altar, the offering, and the fire that receives it.

This path is not for the curious. It is for the committed. There is no glamour here. No robes. No ceremonial applause. There is only the inner flame—and your capacity to hold it.

If you are still drawn to ritual—bless that. Walk that path well. But when the outer forms begin to fade and the inner call grows louder...

Know that the Fire of Mind is already waiting.

And it will burn you into radiance.

The Dangers of Premature Invocation

There is no shortcut to the fire. And those who attempt to seize it before they are ready often find themselves scorched—not because the fire is cruel, but because it is precise. The Fire of Mind is an exacting force. It will burn through anything impure, including the unprepared personality.

Premature invocation often begins not with malice, but with desperation. A seeker, longing for transformation, stumbles upon sacred language or methods and begins to apply them without inner readiness. They invoke the higher without having stabilized the lower. They channel light without having cleared shadow. And in doing so, they create a current they cannot yet ground.

I say this not from theory, but from lived experience. My own early path was littered with spiritual hazards born of this very mistake. In my eagerness to taste the Real, I bypassed safeguards. I pulled in more energy than I could integrate. What followed was not bliss—but fragmentation. The fires of the Soul, when invoked prematurely, become the fires of madness. This is an occult law, not a poetic metaphor.

Some who do this never recover in one lifetime. Others become entangled in grey or black magic, unknowingly using spiritual force for personal ends because they lacked the discernment to feel the difference. The intention may be good—but the result, if unaligned, is still distortion. One does not get to plead innocence before the laws of energy.

Even worse is when the personality enjoys the effects of premature contact: heightened charisma, psychic perception, attraction of followers. This can breed subtle spiritual arrogance—the most dangerous form of illusion. One begins to believe they are the fire, rather than a vessel being prepared to receive it. And from there, the fall is often hard, and humiliating, and absolutely necessary.

The Agni Yogi path requires patience. There is no bypassing the slow burn of purification. It is wiser to invoke less, and integrate more. There is no virtue in intensity without stability. There is no mastery in contact without containment.

So let this be a loving warning:

If you are not sure you are ready, you are not ready.

If you are still ruled by emotional tides, still pulled by glamour or identity—tend to the basics first. Meditation. Harmlessness. Inner discipline. These are not obstacles to the fire. They are its foundation.

Hierarchy will never deny you what you are ready for. But it will also never rush you. The Soul knows your pace. The Masters are not impressed by drama. They look for those who are steady, pure in motive, and willing to wait for the flame to choose them.

W.M.A.

The fire is not a reward.

It is a responsibility.

The Lived Embodiment of Soul Fire

There comes a time when the fire no longer visits—it abides. It no longer descends—it emerges from within. This is not because you have conquered the fire, but because you have become transparent enough for it to remain.

The lived embodiment of Soul Fire is quiet. It is not a constant ecstasy. It is not showy or dramatic. It hums beneath your breath. It sharpens your thoughts. It softens your presence. You find yourself choosing silence more often, not because you lack words, but because the fire speaks better through your being than through your speech.

You begin to notice a reorientation in how you relate to life. Tasks become invocations. Relationships become mirrors. Pain becomes purifying. Time feels less linear. You move not by impulse, but by inner signal. There is no desire to manipulate reality—only to participate in its unfolding, aligned to the higher pattern.

This embodiment is not perfection—it is precision. The Soul is not asking you to ascend out of your humanity, but to illuminate it. The Fire of Mind descends into form not to escape matter, but to redeem it. Every moment becomes an opportunity for radiation. Your body becomes the lamp. Your presence becomes the offering.

You may still feel pain. You may still feel fear. But now, they are seen. Held. Transmuted. The fire does not remove your humanity—it hollows it out until only essence remains. What's left is not some angelic ideal, but a fully human being through whom the Soul can walk.

This is where the path truly begins to shift from personal transformation to planetary service. When the fire has a stable vessel, it begins to use that vessel to shape reality—not by force, but by resonance. You speak little, but your presence reorders the field. You no longer "do magic." You are magic.

This section is only a doorway—an invocation of what it means to live as the flame. What comes next will deepen this further: in energy, in practice, and in mythic truth.

The embodiment of Soul Fire is not a singular moment of arrival—it is a state of sustained contact, renewed daily by your willingness to remain present through each purification. It is less like a final initiation and more like a sunrise that never stops rising. There is always more light. There is always more to see.

You begin to notice that life does not so much happen to you anymore—it begins to happen through you. The distinction is subtle, but seismic. Your thoughts are no longer private ripples—they are radiant lines of force that affect the subtle architecture of the field around you. With every moment of awareness, you become increasingly responsible for the vibration you emit.

This can feel like pressure at first—a weight. But soon you realize it is a blessing. To walk with the fire is to become trustworthy with power. And what greater power is there than love that is directed by will and illuminated by wisdom?

You will also notice the body beginning to respond. The fire affects matter. Subtle alignments in the spine, shifts in the breath, a new rhythm in the pulse—all arise as the physical vehicle becomes more responsive to the energy descending through the Soul. This is not always pleasant. Detoxing old patterning, both physically and etherically, can bring exhaustion, dizziness, even grief. But with every shedding, the body becomes more luminous, more transparent to the Presence.

You become a tuning fork for divine harmony. When you are near others, they feel a pressure to elevate—not because you are better, but because the fire in you stirs the flame in them. This is the radiatory effect of Soul Fire: it awakens others by resonance, not persuasion. Some will draw closer. Some will retreat. Let both responses be holy.

You may also begin to feel less "of this world." Not in detachment or escapism, but in vision. You begin to sense the world as it could be—not in fantasy, but in reality reshaped by the Plan. You feel this possible future in your heart like a secret you're no longer allowed to keep. You want to speak it, live it, write it, share it. This too is part of the embodiment: to make the invisible visible. To incarnate heaven.

The embodied Agni Yogi becomes a living link in the chain of Hierarchy. Not because they are superior, but because they are available. When the fire finds a ready vessel, it flows. And when it flows, others awaken. Systems shift. The veils thin. The world turns quietly toward the Light, even when it doesn't yet know why.

And so your life ceases to be about your story, and becomes about your sound. Your frequency. Your pattern. What you emanate. What you offer. What you leave behind in every room, every word, every silence. This is the final magic.

Not spectacle. Not power.

Presence.

You've walked this far with the fire.

Now let us see where it leads.

W.M.A.

CHAPTER VIII

A VOYAGE THROUGH THE FIRES OF GRIEF

"Grief is the furnace of the heart, where the ashes of suffering become the incense of the soul. Each tear is a rite, each ache a prayer—grief the path, and love the fire that guides it home."

The Path Through Fire: A Transmission in Grief and Light

It is in the high places that I remember peace.
When I walk among the mountains—especially near the still, clear waters—I feel the calm beneath all chaos. Despite losing Him—the only being who ever truly saw me—I find myself wrapped in a strange and ecstatic stillness. A peace that sings beneath the grief, because I know my purpose, even if I do not yet grasp its full shape.

There is something thrilling about incarnation, even now. Something wildly sacred about letting go of control and learning to guide our vessel through waters we cannot still. We do our best to navigate toward the Light— through currents thick with ancestral burdens and the sharp sediment of our own lived trauma. But even these heavy things are holy. The fire that meets us in the depths of our pain is the same fire that clears the path for what we came here to become.

Know this: your ancestors are with you.
They are not watching in judgment, but in awe. They know how rare it is to be fully awake inside a body during such a time as this. They honor your strength, your refusal to go numb, your aching persistence. You are not weak for your wounds. You are the one who stepped forward to heal the bloodline. And that makes you sacred.

So for whatever it's worth—I am proud of you.
Not in the way of platitudes, but in the way that one Soul recognizes another's striving through the veil. You are moving in the right direction, even when the path

dissolves beneath your feet. Especially then. Confusion is not a failure—it is a sacred pause. An initiation.

When you learn to embrace the tides of your life—both the swelling highs and the descending lows—you will find yourself spiraling upward with greater speed than ever before. This is how the Soul travels: not in a straight line, but in the sacred helix of becoming. With each turn of the moon, with each exhale of the Earth, you are brought closer to the core of your purpose.

The Moon brings more than mystery—She brings gentle clarity. Her phases echo your own cycles. Her waning teaches release. Her waxing teaches receptivity. And through her reflection, we are reminded of the greater fire —the blazing heart of the Solar Logos, the sacred sun from which all vitality flows.

This Great Star is not merely a light in the sky. It is the mind of the Logos, the radiant emanation of divine intelligence, and the unceasing wellspring of life. It is from this Solar Body that we are gifted the fire of knowing, the breath of continuity, the very substance of our awareness. Every breath you take is a prayer returned from that central flame. Call on it. Call Him to guide you, to anchor you, to illumine the Way beneath your feet.

Let that light burn through you—not with violence, but with truth.
Let it remind you who you are, and whose you are.

Realize that every word, and the way that I write, is intentional.

Despite the conventions of grammar, my fluctuations stand as keys. They are codes—signals for the intuitive mind. They are part of a language whispered through time by the ancient ones, by the occultists, by those who saw with the Eye and wrote for Souls, not for surface comprehension. If you train yourself to pause at these markings—to meditate upon them—you will begin to decode the deeper rhythm behind this text and others like it. This is how one learns to read esoterically.

Do not assume that occult texts like The Secret Doctrine were meant to be understood by the intellect alone. They require the Light of the Soul to be opened. They require vibration, not just interpretation. Ponder this deeply and let it settle into your meditative awareness.

I repeat this affirmation often—many times throughout the day—as a mantra for my life and my mission:
"Everything is working out for me as I work toward alignment with Who it is that I Am."

All things—yes, all things—begin to fall into right alignment when my mind, my astral heart, and my physical body move into harmony with the Light of the Solar Angel. This is the Source within me, the radiant intermediary between my personality and my divine essence. This Light holds the memory of my vow and the blueprint of my path.

I am not here by chance.

I am here to fulfill a mission of divine origin—to walk the Way of ecstatic Light.

The Way of Entheo Lux—the inner illumination that connects all worlds through the radiant fire of the Source. This fire pours forth from the Silent Center, that Great Life in whom we live, move, and have our being.

And I am One with that Life.

Nothing—no darkness, no failure, no death—can sever that bond.

As the Antahkarana is being woven by the New Group of World Servers, alongside the tireless work of the Devas who build with Light, the bridge is forming—between this world and the great Centers of Hierarchy and Shamballa. With every act of alignment, we strengthen the cords. With every meditation rightly performed, we thicken the strand.

We are preparing for the externalization of Hierarchy and the Reappearance of the Christ. But He will not appear unless we prepare the Way. He will not violate the sacred law of Free Will. It rests on our shoulders to resolve the crisis of Right Human Relations. It is our responsibility to build the container for His return.

Through the Fires of Mind, we can bring forth the conditions needed to receive Him. The world must be remade in Light—not through revolution of blood, but through revolution of consciousness.

This is significant.
This is cosmic.

What is happening now is not just a shift in human awareness—it is the initiation of the planetary Logos. The Earth itself is beginning to enter a higher spiral, drawing ever closer to sacredness. When this initiation is complete, our world will join the ranks of planets like Venus and Saturn—planets whose auras pulse with divine beauty and equilibrium. The rays impacting Earth are shifting. And as they do, the vibrational field of this entire solar system changes.

It is not just humanity that evolves.
The galaxy watches. The stars respond.
This is a turning point not only for Earth, but for every consciousness touched by its song.

My grandmother used to tell me:
"When you're writing, let the words come out first. Fix them later."
I've never forgotten that.

It is perhaps the most important piece of advice I ever received about creation. There is no need to dam the river of inspiration just to polish the stones on the riverbed. That can come later, when the waters have calmed. But during the flood of revelation—during those fragile moments when Spirit pours through you like fire in your bones—write. Let it be wild. Let it be messy. Let it be real. Truth doesn't need a clean page. It needs an open channel.

So I say to you: write what you feel, speak what you know, and let the structure come in time. What matters most is the integrity of your inner flame.

And I want to repeat what may be the most important truth in this whole transmission:
You are blessed, even in the dark.
Especially in the dark.

When the night is long and the world seems to turn against your efforts—that is when the Light is closest. That is when Hierarchy leans in, watching, waiting, rejoicing quietly at the Soul's realization:
"My obstacles are my initiations."

Practice believing that, and you will discover the gold hidden inside even your worst moments. I am not theorizing—I am living proof. I have faced storms I thought would destroy me. I have walked blindly through fire and felt it blister my mind. But I chose to walk with courageous, righteous intention, and every time I did, the darkness transmuted into Light.

There is no more rewarding way to walk the Path.

Through failure, we find success.
Through descent, we access the core.
Through darkness, we learn to see Light as it truly is—not a soft glow, but a fire that consumes illusion.

Be wary of the false teachings that say Light comes only by resisting darkness. This is inversion. The Light does not banish the dark by denial—it transforms it by witness. It heals by integration. The Soul shines through like starlight through the veil of space—visible only when we stop fearing the night.

If you struggle with lack, if the pain of "not enough" haunts your days—halt those thoughts. Pause them. Disrupt them. And in their place, let gratitude rise. Even if it feels forced at first, give thanks for what you do have, no matter how small. Gratitude is the opening gate through which greater abundance flows.

But do not confuse this with passivity. The Path requires work. Sacred work. You are not being asked to "love and light" your way through suffering—you are being asked to forge gold from it. To shape it with your Will. And yes, the work is hard. But I promise you: every word I write here is a map. If you read them rightly, the Way will begin to emerge beneath your feet.

I say this with reverence and humility:
It is only because I have walked this Path beside you that I can carry the knowing I now hold.

Whatever I have to offer, it does not come from theory. It comes from experience. I do not speak as an authority above you—I speak as a student who may be just a few paces ahead, reaching back with a steady hand to help you avoid the most dangerous traps I once fell into. I am not proud of my missteps, but I am grateful for what they forged in me. They sharpened my Will. They clarified my Devotion. They made real the Work I once only believed in.

There were moments I was swallowed whole.
Moments I made choices so harmful—so karmically heavy —that I could not see how I might return to the Light. The grief was unspeakable. The darkness, total. My own mind

became unfamiliar terrain. I do not wish to expand on the full depths of those experiences—not now. But I will say this:

I survived by making my suffering sacred.

I made a vow that if I had to endure it, it would not be in vain.
My body became a Temple of Suffering, and I dedicated it wholly to the service of Humanity. Every tear became a libation. Every psychic wound, a portal to compassion. I learned that the Laws of Suffering and Equalization are not cruel—they are precise. They are mathematical. And they are holy.

Would I take those years back?
Not for anything.
Not even to erase the pain.
Those years were a gift.

As strange as it may sound, it was only through the utter collapse of my former life that I found the doorway into the Real. It was only through dissolution that the foundation for my deeper Self could be poured. This is not poetic metaphor—it is esoteric fact. The structure of the Soul must be constructed through sacrifice. And I would walk through it again, knowing now what was waiting on the other side.

"I reach into the silent place, and bring from thence the Gift of Understanding…
I reach up into the Light, and bring it down to meet the need."

This invocation is not just a verse—it is a technology. A mechanism of Soul-directed will. A call-and-response between planes. When you suffer, say it. When you are confused, say it. When you begin to crack open under the pressure of this world, say it—and feel yourself become a conduit once more.

Understand that the Light is not gentle. It is not soft and safe and pastel.
The Light, when truly contacted, burns. It sears away illusion.
And this is precisely why the false religious forms, the cults of external salvation—what I call Churchianity—have taught the opposite. They say the Light is comfort, and that darkness is to be feared. But they speak from inversion.

These religions, for all their outer piety, have become one of the most dangerous expressions of the Dark Lodge on Earth. They claim to mediate Divinity, but in truth, they separate you from it. They promise salvation, but they fracture you from the truth of your own indwelling Flame.

And it is that separation—the lie of distance from Source —that creates the very suffering they claim to cure.

It is time to confront the misaligned paradigms that have governed human understanding for too long.
In particular, we must examine one of the most insidious: the widespread acceptance of entropy as absolute law.

The prevailing scientific doctrine tells us that all systems inevitably decay, that chaos increases over time, and that life is a brief flicker against the backdrop of an ever-dissolving cosmos. This interpretation of entropy has shaped not just physics—it has infiltrated our worldview. It tells the soul: You are temporary. You are powerless. You are alone in a dying machine.

But the Ageless Wisdom teaches another reality. A higher law.
One known not to the laboratories of materialism, but to the initiates of the flame.

Order is the true nature of the universe.
Not the fragile, temporary order of man-made systems—but the living, breathing Order that unfolds through Hierarchy. A divine pattern radiates outward from the Central Spiritual Sun, and everything responds to its rhythm. Decay is not a collapse into nothingness—it is transmutation. It is the reorganization of matter, energy, and consciousness into higher alignment with the Will of the Whole.

What appears as breakdown is, in truth, refinement.
Destruction serves Creation when seen from above.

We must begin to understand that what modern science calls "disorder" is actually the preparation of the field for reseeding. That which seems chaotic from below is often exquisitely patterned from a higher dimension. This is one of the core laws of occultism: that any system, when viewed from the appropriate plane, reveals its inner symmetry.

Let us now name the Being whose principle governs this process:

Vishnu—the Preserver. The Upholder. The Sustainer of Cosmic Rhythm.

In the Hindu teaching, Vishnu is the divine force that maintains the universe against collapse. He does not prevent transformation—but He ensures continuity through it. His work is subtle, constant, quiet. And it is His energy that moves through what occultism calls the Second Aspect of Divinity: Love-Wisdom. The magnetic cohesion of form around purpose.

When you experience stability after crisis, that is Vishnu.
When you see cycles within chaos, that is Vishnu.
When you intuit that something sacred holds the center while everything changes, that is Vishnu.

The Western world, in its pursuit of objective knowledge, has forgotten Him. And in doing so, it has forgotten the true spiritual dimension of science. The Third Ray—the Ray of Active Intelligence, which governs human scientific endeavor—was meant to be aligned with Divine Purpose. But in the absence of spiritual direction, it was distorted. It became what we see now: a pursuit of control, not communion. Dissection, not revelation.

But the tides are shifting.

As the Seventh Ray gains strength in this Aquarian Age, science will be reborn—not as cold analysis, but as Ceremonial Order. Magic will return—not the theatrics of illusion, but the sacred science of energetic causality, practiced with harmlessness and governed by Love. The

Devas—those angelic builders of form—will no longer be ignored. The etheric web of the Earth will be mapped and tended with reverence. And those once labeled "occultists" will be understood as engineers of the subtle realms, restoring balance between humanity, nature, and the planetary Logos.

We are not heading toward chaos. We are returning to alignment.

The illusion of entropy is dissolving.
And in its place, the spiral of spiritual progress becomes visible once more.

Humanity is not spiraling downward.
We are being drawn upward by the very laws we have forgotten.
And those of us who walk the Path in service know this:
We are not resisting collapse.
We are preparing the blueprint for resurrection.

W.M.A.

The Initiator

Deepen your connection to the Teacher—by any means possible.

He does not dwell in books.
He does not hide in temples built by hands.
He lives in the sanctum of your own heart.
He is present in the center of every triangle formed in service. He radiates from the core of Hierarchy, where Love-Wisdom flows like fire in stillness. He is not a distant symbol. He is alive within you—waiting for recognition, for rhythm, for approach.

He goes by many names across the ages.
The Christ. Maitreya. The World Teacher.
He is not owned by any religion. He is not the exclusive property of dogma. He is a Flame that has walked among us again and again, through countless incarnations, always guiding, always watching, always preparing humanity to remember its Divinity.

And now, once more, He prepares to return.

But He will not descend as an interruption.
He comes when the field is ready—when humanity, of its own free will, begins to walk in rhythm with Right Relations and global cooperation. That is why our work matters. That is why discipleship is needed now more than ever. We are not waiting for a savior. We are co-creating the space through which He may reappear.

The Age of Aquarius is upon us. But Aquarius does not stand alone.
Behind it moves Capricornus, the great Initiator.

Capricorn brings the structure, the discipline, the mountaintop vision required to embody the Aquarian dream. It governs the Science of Initiation, the inner architecture of the Path, the climb from instinct to intellect to intuition and finally into Illumination. And it is this energy that we, as teachers and servants, must study—must align with—so that when we turn from the Light, we turn only to radiate it outward.

I speak now to the seekers just awakening:
You are not late. You are not underqualified. The very fact that you are reading these words means the magnet of the Soul has stirred. Listen to that call. Do not rush. Do not seek hierarchy in outer things. Seek it in inner coherence. Begin with harmlessness. Let your thoughts become sacred. Train your attention as if it were fire—because it is.

And I speak to the seasoned disciples, many of whom have walked the Path longer than I:
Do not grow weary. Do not allow fatigue to disguise itself as humility. This is a time of activation. We are not being asked to hide in our sanctuaries—we are being asked to build new ones, out in the world, in full view. The Work must go public. The science of the Soul must be reborn through new forms—through education, through healing technologies, through spiritual governance and cultural architecture.

The day is fast approaching when all of this—every word you read here—will be measurable, replicable, observable. The field of science is shifting. The Seventh Ray is rising. And through it, the mystical will become empirical—not because it becomes less sacred, but because humanity will have evolved to the point where it can hold the sacred in its systems.

This is why we write.
This is why we serve.
Not to be seen—but to plant the future in the minds of those who are ready.

And so I leave you here, for now.
But not without a final breath:

You are not alone.
You are not broken.
You are part of a Plan so radiant, so exact, so beautiful—
That when the veils finally lift, you will not fall to your knees in fear.
You will rise in joy, and say, "Of course. Of course it was always this."

W.M.A.

The Veil, the Fire, and the Rising Light

Our individual roles in this physical world require us to remain present to the tangibility of glamour—that much is basic and clear. I'm not telling you something you don't already know. Yet even within the busiest of lives, each of us is offered the chance to go inward, to cultivate awareness of what lies just behind the veil. Enough has been uncovered about the nervous system to suggest that it is a lattice of living rivers—carriers of electric fire, woven through flesh and will. The average person may still believe this system functions outside of conscious influence, but that is not entirely true—and is certainly not the case for those who have awakened to their inner life.

The most important phenomena for spiritual development at this stage of evolution involve the subtle currents flowing upward from the base of the spine to the brain, terminating in the master gland—the pituitary—which is magnetically linked to the pineal gland. The pineal gland, encased in crystalline calcite structures, becomes increasingly responsive when activated through disciplined occult meditation. These crystals, when charged, begin to generate a subtle magnetic field—a pulsation that marks the unfolding of the auric life. I wrote about this in my last book, and I return to it here to say: this is not metaphor. This is not symbolic. It is an experience, and it is repeatable.

This magnetic pulsation strengthens as one's subtle currents are refined, and as they do, the so-called "supernatural" gifts of the Soul begin to manifest. But I must be clear: there is nothing supernatural about them. There is nothing that exists outside of what is natural. The more accurate term is supernormal—a reference to that which lies latent within the fullness of the human design, awaiting activation.

This experience is not abstract. It is not poetic fancy. It is fact—and has been recorded and shared by humanity across thousands of years. What has kept it hidden is not the rarity of its occurrence, but the sacred veils surrounding its method of attainment. The signs and keys to this process are all around us, embedded in story, art, architecture, music, dreams, and tradition. But only those truly aspiring to the Path are willing to allow these symbols to speak. That is part of the Law. It has always been so.

And yet, something has changed. As the symbols of the Sacred penetrate even the densest corners of this planetary sphere, a great call is sounding for the multitude of sleeping souls to rise—to trek the Path of Discipleship and ultimately stand before the Gates of Initiation. It is a call that must be answered freely and in love, without coercion or fear, and only by those who hear it with their inner ear.

Now, in the twenty-first century, we are approaching a threshold where scientific instrumentation is finally sensitive enough to measure the energetic phenomena that mystics and initiates have always known. This is an exciting moment. As the occidental mind gradually awakens to the profound truth of consciousness, magnetic fields, and their role in shaping physical reality, humanity will take its first stride toward the Golden Era.

But let us not forget: those of us who already walk this Path must be vigilant. There is danger in haste, especially now. We must be ready to teach, to guide, and to protect those seekers who may attempt to race ahead without discipline, humility, or understanding. The Age of Pisces conditioned humanity to seek spiritual recognition through separation, through competition, and through the subtle glamour of "being chosen." That age is closing. We now enter the Aeon of Group Cohesion, of goodwill, and of spiritual synergy. These are cornerstones of the New World Order—not the distorted vision feared by the masses, but the Hierarchically inspired blueprint of planetary integration and peace.

Competition among nations, still dominant in scientific research and global policy, stands as a final echo of the outgoing age. Why should the brightest minds be isolated from one another in secrecy and fear? Why should scientific discovery be driven by rivalry and resource control rather than cooperation and common good? These questions are meant not only to be pondered—but acted upon.

As the tides of war recede and the new energies continue anchoring, we will witness a profound shift in the focus of scientific and medical advancement. Fields once dismissed as fringe—energy medicine, consciousness studies, frequency healing—will become central to our collective transformation. I cannot overstate the importance of investigating the subtle realms of causal energy. The sooner we do, the sooner we will unlock the secrets of radiant health, energetic regeneration, and peace on Earth.

I am the one who seeks the Way. I am the disciple who has found the Way. I am the accepted disciple who knows the Way. I am the initiate who has become the Way.
I am a server seeking to serve. I am the White Magician of Ceremonial Order. I am the Agni Yogi who is Fire.

Personal Reflection

Lately, I've begun setting aside sacred time for myself— time to simply sit, breathe, and let my consciousness flow freely into these pages. No pressure. No expectations. Just the quiet act of writing as worship, as offering, as devotion. This is my sacred joy: to express what lives within me and share it with those who may someday be touched by these words. My prayer is that it serves the Plan and honors the Hierarchy.

I've found a place that feels like home—a mountain refuge where water glistens, fir trees breathe, and the sky is wide and alive. It's in this place that I remember: I am not running out of time. I am running into it. With it. Beyond it. Every perceived ending has only ever been a beginning in disguise. And this... this is my beginning.

The more I allow my thoughts to funnel through me into form, the closer I come to fulfilling my purpose—and, paradoxically, the closer I draw to dispassion. I no longer fear that the world will hear or read what I've kept hidden inside. For years I resisted this work. Maybe it's truer to say the work resisted me, gently demanding that I wait, that I grow strong enough to hold it.

As I write, I learn. As I teach, I seek to be taught. And as I seek, I find new language for the old truths whispering in my Soul.

This is how I participate in the New Group of World Servers. This is how I step into higher service. Through writing, I find clarity. Through writing, I remember who I am.

W.M.A.

The Spiral and the Structure

Every system in nature thrives through hierarchy. This is not a doctrine of dominance—it is the law of ordered becoming. From the smallest expressions of life to the vast celestial forms, all things evolve by ascending turns of the spiral. Hierarchy is not imposed from above; it is emergent, intrinsic, and ever-unfolding. It is the natural rhythm of ascent.

Look closely and this truth is self-evident. Atoms gather into molecules, which combine into cellular structures, which form tissues, which organize into organs and systems, creating the living body. As above, so below: galaxies spin around centers of force, and even nations are held together by systems of energetic coherence, whether visible or invisible. This pattern—of integration and refinement—applies not only to matter, but to consciousness.

This is why the Ageless Wisdom recognizes the presence of a latent soul evolving through all forms: from the mineral kingdom to the vegetable, from the animal into the human, and onward into what we call the Kingdom of Heaven. That term may sound poetic or distant, but it simply refers to a plane of higher realization—a state wherein the human being steps into the form and function of Godman: the conscious co-creator. Beyond this threshold lie mysteries yet untold, and we will not explore them here. For now, we focus on the bridge—on the steps that carry us from personality to Soul, from separateness into divine synthesis.

Human society, too, reflects this pattern. From governments to corporations, from spiritual groups to families, all operate on hierarchical structure—ideally not as systems of control, but as systems of coordinated service. Let us widen the lens further: what if these visible structures are but shadows of a greater, subtler system? What if a planetary Hierarchy—composed of lives far more advanced than ourselves—has long guided human evolution from behind the veil?

This is no fantasy. For those who begin to resonate with the Light of their own Souls, the reality of Hierarchy becomes palpable. When one aligns with the currents of the Group Light, the presence of those guiding forces becomes undeniable. These lives—these Masters of the Wisdom—never interfere with our free will, but they do offer guidance, protection, and illumination when the disciple becomes ready. It is not their role to intervene uninvited; it is our role to respond to their vibration and to externalize the Plan here on Earth through service, goodwill, and right relations.

That work—the externalization of Hierarchy and the anchoring of the New World Order—is not a far-off prophecy. It is a process already underway. Yes, the phrase "New World Order" has been hijacked by the fearful and distorted by those who operate in the shadows. But we reclaim it here for what it truly means: the dawning of an age of synthesis, of unity, of sacred cooperation among all peoples and nations under spiritual law.

Those who cling to outdated power structures, or who claim to be orchestrating this "order" through cabals of control, are simply enacting the final gestures of the dying world. They are not the builders of the new age—they are the dust from which the new will rise. The Great Inversion may still enchant many minds, but its spell is weakening. We are witnessing a planetary transformation—one that moves us from fear into empathy, from division into communion.

And who are the harbingers of this change? The youth. The incoming souls of this era have arrived carrying keys. Their moral clarity, their instinctive tolerance, their desire for equality and justice—these are signs of karmic preparation. These are souls ready to serve, to innovate, and to break the old paradigms open with radiant light. I have witnessed it again and again: children standing with ancient wisdom in their eyes, their voices rising in defense of Earth, of love, of truth.

The most essential task for the seeker is to locate the activity that generates the most love within you. What stirs your fire? What aligns your breath and bones to something higher? This is your opening—your way into the Work. It may begin as an art, a study, a devotion, or a whisper. Whatever form it takes, follow it, refine it, and offer it. The rest will come. Discipleship is not imposed from above; it is accepted inwardly and earned through service.

Let me be transparent: I do not hold myself as a model of perfection. I still stumble. I still fall for glamour and illusion. But I strive, and I surrender again each day. I share my thoughts not as dogma, but as a personal testament to the Path. I do not want to be looked up to—I only ask to be looked into, with understanding. These are my truths, and I offer them in good faith. If they spark something in you, let them live on.

I know well that these words may invite controversy. Some may deem me heretical. If the doctrines of "churchianity" condemn me, I accept that with peace. I have seen too clearly the mechanisms by which false religion seeks to control the soul—how it reduces spiritual truth into fear and compliance, cloaking divine sovereignty in shame and separation. That age is ending. That veil is lifting.

The soul I serve flows from peace. But my personality, aligned with that soul, burns with the Will to enact change. I work with the First Ray of Power, and that energy—though often misunderstood—is not destructive for its own sake. It is the fire that clears the field, the sword that severs the ties of tyranny. Many of you who are drawn to these pages work with this same ray. You know its pulse. You feel its call. It is not the fire of violence—it is the fire of sacred disruption.

If you have been practicing prescribed occult meditation within a trusted tradition or school, I trust that you are beginning to feel this power stirring within you. You are not powerless. You are not insignificant. The current that flows through you connects you to the great Ashrams of the Masters, to the collective field of the Group Soul. If your intentions are pure and your seeking is true, you will not be misled.

This is especially true for the rising generations. I hold no fear for their future, because I sense the codes they carry. Their clarity is piercing. Their hearts are vast. They have not come to repeat history—they have come to rewrite it.

And so, we must begin to look toward the larger stage. As international bodies—such as the United Nations and its branches, the World Court, the World Bank, and others— begin to evolve and take shape under Hierarchical inspiration, we are witnessing the early scaffolding of planetary stewardship. These organizations, for all their current flaws, are seeds of a united humanity. They are not to be feared but refined.

This is the true New World Order—not of control, but of cohesion. Not a shadow government, but a dawning alignment. A system ruled not by fear or profit, but by principles streaming down from Shamballa itself. When one walks in alignment with Infinity, fear dissolves. As it has been said: "There is nothing to fear but fear itself." Fear is the final stronghold of separation—the last illusion to fall before the soul rises in its fullness.

There is no place for a divided humanity in our planetary evolution. I invite you to release every strand of separative thinking—religious, political, cultural, or otherwise. If a belief system teaches you to condemn, it is false. If a system demands that you shrink, it is false. If an institution claims that you must access God only through it, it is false.

Let those cords fall. Or they will be cut—by your own soul, in due time.

This is not a threat. It is simply the Law of Return—the Great Equalizer. The Truth will be faced. The Light will rise. The only question is: Will you walk toward it, or be carried to it?

Either way, beloved—you are going home.

W.M.A.

The Fire That Purifies

The tasks ahead of you require nothing less than a fearless, soul-integrated approach. They will not pause for your hesitation. They will not wait for your convenience. The momentum of evolution continues, with or without your participation. This is not spoken to incite fear, but to spark remembrance. You are needed. Your light is needed. Your alignment matters—not just to you, but to the Whole.

My only hope is that you, dear seeker, have awakened from the long dream of the reigning darkness—that you are no longer under its spell. If you are still half-asleep, then hear this: your soul will not allow slumber to last forever. Not in this age. Not with this fire streaming forth into the world. As your supernormal faculties develop, as your inner senses unfold, the darkness that once seemed overwhelming begins to dissolve in your presence. Your very auric field becomes a torch of transmutation, a living flame through which distortion is burned away—often without your conscious awareness.

This is the silent miracle of the Path.

And is it not curious that the inverted orders of the world —particularly the dogmas of churchianity—have turned fire into a symbol of punishment? That they have threatened us with the very element that is the essence of liberation?

Fire is Life.

All light is born of fire—whether it be electric fire, solar fire, or the radiant Fire of Mind. This was addressed in my previous work, and I will continue to expand upon it here, including supplemental articles and writings. But for now, hold this esoteric truth close to your heart: Fire stands behind all the elements, even Water.

This is not metaphor. It is occult fact.

Consider the atom—not as a mechanistic structure, but as a conscious unit. Consider the electric fire within each electron, the spiraling dance of subtle energy binding it to its neighbors. If the atom is alive, then all matter is alive. And if fire lives at the core of every atom, then fire lives at the core of all being. It is the divine intermediary between spirit and form.

The time has come to let go of the past—not as a poetic idea, but as an act of power. The burdens you've carried: the shame, the regret, the endless self-recriminations— they are kindling. Offer them to the sacred flame. Let Fire and Water cleanse you.

Let them wash through you until only clarity remains.

All of it—every misstep, every sorrow—brought you to this moment. That is the only part of your past that matters now. It brought you here. And here, you are being led toward harmlessness, toward perfect alignment with your Solar Angel, and toward an unimpeded descent of Light into your being.

You are becoming the bridge.

And what stands in your way? Only that which you refuse to release.

All harm committed—knowingly or unknowingly—must be forgiven, released, and transmuted in the Light. This is not to say that responsibility is erased. It is to say that you are no longer meant to remain bound by psychic residue. The future calls. It always has. Even the "present moment," in the strictest sense, is already the past— perceived only after it has passed through time's veil. So let your gaze tilt forward. Let your body live now as if it already dwells in the world to come.

If you are striving toward the better, more luminous self— then know this: you will not be left behind. The soul waits for no one, but it also forsakes no one. You have eternity to walk this Path, but oh, what a time it is to walk it now! The gates are open. The energies flooding the planet are unprecedented. To ignore this opportunity is not sin, but it is loss. Choose wisely.

You are immersed in currents—within your body and without—that flow whether or not you are aware of them. The rivers of life move always. But now imagine the strength of those waters when your consciousness joins them. Imagine your awareness as rain falling into the current, feeding the stream, enhancing its depth and direction. This is how your inner life contributes to the Group Work.

It matters.

Even if you feel small. Even if all you can do is sit quietly and breathe light into the world. That is enough. That is service.

The soul does not measure effort by grandeur. It measures by alignment.

This is why the Work of occult meditation is so vital now —not simply as a private spiritual practice, but as a planetary act. The more each one of us strengthens these inner channels, the more those energies circulate through the collective pool of humanity. One meditation, rightly performed, can affect the unseen structure of the whole. You are not just a person praying. You are a cell in the Heart of the Earth, pulsing with rhythmic will.

If you can do nothing else—do this.

Sit. Be still. Listen. Observe the Light behind your breath. Feel its expansion through your heart. Trace its current as it joins with the light of others in the web of humanity. Know that this subtle act helps build the bridge between worlds.

In this way, even the quietest soul becomes a builder of the new age.

W.M.A.

The Threshold Approaches

The time is drawing near. For those of us who came prepared—who woke ourselves up early, despite the cost, the danger, and the consequences on both physical and mental planes—the transition is nearly complete. We knew, long ago, that the dangers would become our greatest teachers. And so, in the absence of guides, it was danger itself that became our guide. The descent into the unknown forged our ascent.

The dangers are plentiful, yes—but there is beauty in their complexity. For every intricate trap we stumble into (often ones we ourselves set in the beginning), there are countless strength-testing routes toward escape, toward victory. In my heart, I truly believe that the perils of life can be among its most joyous and adventurous moments. There is no sin in a soul willing to fall—so long as it knows it will rise again.

For every scar, a story. For every bruise, a glorious tumble. Without my mistakes, I would be but a shallow, stagnant well—tidy, but lifeless. So I revel in my errors and try, always, to shape from each a living parable.

And what of love? Is it ever truly a mistake?

When two wounded souls come together—wild, raw, unguarded—fighting to heal, but still uncertain of how to do so... when that alchemy turns chaotic and spirals into toxicity, can it be rightly called a mistake? I think not. I wouldn't take back a single moment of the madness. Of course, there are things I regret—words I wish I hadn't spoken, shadows I wish I hadn't fed. But still… I miss him. I miss everything. Even the storm of it.

He brought me to life. He filled me with a fire that illuminated my aura from within. And though I tried so often to battle his shadows, I rarely gave him credit for the brilliance of his Light. Now, I don't know if I'll ever get the chance to. But I hope. I hope I will.

Deep within my core, I know that love—pure and peaceful—will return to me. And until it does, I will fight for myself. I will build something beautiful, something enduring, something that I can one day offer freely and without fear. The truth is, I had never truly chosen myself before—not until this past year. Not until the void. And in choosing myself, I finally opened the gates of my own love.

Though the battle in my mind still flickers, it no longer consumes me. The voice of peace grows louder. The path grows clearer.

There is still so much goodness ahead. Despite the seemingly endless nights spent waiting for a sunrise that never seemed to come, I now know: the sun is rising. I can feel it. And nothing I do can stop it. Even my missteps serve as lanterns. Every stumble, every detour, leads to that same ancient threshold—the one that will open, inevitably, to what has always been promised.

And so I will keep going. I will endure the burn. I will rise from every fall, carrying with me the sacred vow that my suffering has not been in vain. I have dedicated my pain to those who came before, and to those who will come after—so that they may not have to suffer quite the same.

I owe myself many things. But most of all, I owe myself grace. And so, grace I will give.

The days ahead are radiant. I feel them in my bones.

So I wait—patiently—for the dawning of the New Day and the rising of the New Order. And I know, with quiet certainty, that I am ready to play whatever role I must. Hallelujah.

—

It is so clear to me now that the things I once spoke of, the visions I once whispered into pages over a decade ago, have come to pass. The culmination—the climactic turning point—is directly on the horizon. It will arrive swiftly, and with such brilliance that many will not have time to resist or second-guess its goodness.

I see it clearly now, just as I always have. But I have spent so many years silencing my own intuition, doubting the clarity of my inner knowing, and holding back from speaking what I know to be true. And so—for now—I do not feel the urge to shout it aloud. I do not feel the need to argue. I am here to share through stillness, through presence. My heart is open. That is enough.

My voice, when it rises, will rise through the written word. That has always been my truest offering.

In the last year, I have written more than in the entire previous decade combined, in a voice that I didn't even know I had. And for now, that is enough. It is enough to carry the teachings, the grief, the fire, and the love all into one unfolding expression of service.

The events soon to unfold will be objectively good—but interpretation will vary. Groups will split and fracture over their meanings, just as they do now. The truth, as always, will be distorted by those still ensnared in the glamour of false narratives.

The tides of evolution are here. They are moving rapidly across the face of humanity. And yet, many remain lost— deceived by the age-old masquerade of darkness in the guise of Light. This is not entirely their fault. The Dark Brotherhood has spent millennia weaving a narrative that is deeply compelling, nearly all-encompassing.

But even that veil is thinning.

The Light is rising through the cracks. And what has been hidden will be revealed.

W.M.A.

I Carry You With Me Into Eternity

It is only when I am surrounded by the purity of nature that I feel your presence without question—without doubt or fear. My heart seems to break more and more with each passing day, continually reaching depths of love and sorrow that I had never known before. I hear you telling me that I will be okay, that I will find my way back to you. But right now, it is hard for me to believe that completely. I hear you telling me to write—to let myself connect to the Divine and allow it to flow through my fingertips and into print. Now, more than ever before, I know that is my greatest purpose and what I must do to be with you again. I have already begun, and I will not stop until my purpose is fulfilled.

I will follow my heart and do what I must to achieve the freedom required to fulfill my duties—to pray for humanity, for the planet, and to spread the wisdom I am able to channel into the center we call the human race. This grief... this longing to be where you are... the only people who could begin to understand it are those who have also experienced the loss of their twin flame. Losing you has cemented the truth that this journey is deeply personal for each soul—that even between twin flames, our paths through this dream are unique and sacred. We each descend into this realm for the most deeply spiritual of purposes.

I was blessed to have a love like yours while enduring this life—blessed that the Goddess ensured our union before one of us had to go. I just always thought it would be me to leave first. Even through my fears, I never truly believed this could happen... that it was even remotely a real possibility. But since you've been gone, you've already unlocked a multitude of doors within my mind. You've enhanced my conscious understanding of the Whole—of the dream—of what it means to wake from this dream.

For as much as I do not want to be here without you, I know that I must continue. I must allow my purpose to flow through me so that I don't have to come back again —so that I can be with you for eternity upon waking from this life. And so, that is what I will do.

It is from the Heavens that we descend—into the journey of our soul's plan for growth—to bring the soul's purpose to Earth. And it is into Heaven that we may glimpse some understanding of this purpose while we are still here. Life is a circle, and it is to Heaven that we will all inevitably return, bringing back information and experience. Upon the awakening of the body and mind to the reality of the Soul, we remember that our fuller selves exist in a state of timelessness—that we will, in time, be delivered into the arms of our loved ones who have completed their own journeys. And for those who still have a few more lifetimes to live, it seems we only awaken briefly before they do, because timelessness exists—even though time is still recognized and measured, to some extent, on every plane and in every dimension. It simply becomes far less important once we are no longer caught in the dream of flesh and blood.

The subtle realm still operates within materialistic frequencies. In truth, there is only one essential law: that all comes from—and returns to—a state of oneness and understanding. This includes eternity and immortality, and all Truth may be seen as growing from this foundational law, like branches from the Tree of Life.

I hear you telling me that everything will work out—that I will be free to live out my purpose as comfortably as possible, in a way that allows me to feel close to you as often as I need. I can see that path unfolding in my heart and mind. I hear you telling me that it is through trusting the process, through trusting divine guidance, that I will find my way back to you—that I will step into the life my heart knows I need. It just all feels so heavy without you here on Earth with me.

And if I'm being transparent and honest—there is not a single part of me that wants to be here without you. To have found you after a lifetime of seeking the kind of love you embodied, and then to have lost you... there is no greater pain I could imagine. I made so many mistakes. I said so many things I did not mean. How am I supposed to continue without you, Tyler? What am I supposed to do when all I was ever doing was waiting for you to come back to me? How do I move forward when I can't help but wish that I had died too?

Even with all of my understandings of the Ageless Wisdom —and the implications of eternity beyond this brief, often brutal human life—I think I will always feel that way.

These past few months have melted away with such rapidity that I am left dazed, dissociated, and confused by the circumstances in which I now find myself. I feel as though I'm falling upwards through a spiral over which I have no control, and I am doing my best to trust the steps my feet are being guided to take. I remain in a state of defiant indifference—because no matter how well I perform, none of it will bring you back to the body I loved so dearly.

I am still struggling, intensely, with letting go of my body's physical love for you—allowing my body to truly grieve the loss of yours. Even at such great spiritual heights, your absence in this physical realm makes no sense to my body or my personality. My soul, however, is right there next to yours. And for now, knowing that is what keeps me breathing.

Things are progressing and changing, as they should. I've been learning to remove the "I" more often—learning to surrender to what makes sense in each moment, and to allow space for natural responsiveness from the Soul. That doesn't mean things are unfolding exactly how I would like them to—but I trust that the Universe has things in store for me that I cannot yet see.

An incredibly profound loss is leading to profound change—even in ways that feel familiar, and in others that will feel entirely new. My system is still in shock. I must be honest—I never imagined I would lose him. But this too shall pass... like life itself, an endless stream flowing into infinity—through physical journeys and into timeless space.

And it is there that he waits for me. I will always know that to be true, no matter what.

"We all bow at the feet of the Great Goddess.
We know our own smaller godhood,
but we know when and how to respect those Higher Beings
whose sacrifice and suffering paved the way
for the structuring laws that guide us
further along the Way of transcendent understanding."

They are honored in a way far more exalted than is possible on the physical plane. We See them in higher clarity—and in that seeing, we recognize the truth of their being. They lead us ever upward, back toward the One radiating at the center of the Infinite. Their wisdom returns, like rivers of fire and memory, flowing into the Great Central Mind. And this One... this radiant Source... is far beyond the capacity of any earthly mind to fully grasp.

M.G.S.

And, if it weren't for all I've learned and the strength I've gained along the way, I would think I ended up right back where I started...the fool at the beginning of his journey.

I can't say what's next, but it's always going to be an awe-filled adventure.

The Moment and the Auric Fountain

There is only this moment.

This has been repeated by every Teacher, every Disciple, every Master of the Wisdom—again and again through the ages. And still, it must be said, until it is known. It is here, and only here, that the infinite makes contact with the finite, that the Eternal pierces through the veil of time.

It is only by participating fully in the sanctity of the present that we may move consciously into infinity together. I am grateful to meet you Here, in your Moment. It is in this sacred Now that our unified attention finds steady ground—the luminous footing necessary to transmute us into fully conscious participants in the Work being done in the Far Off Worlds.

We are not only students of Light—we are its conduits.

Our shared mission is to anchor, transmit, and reverberate with the subtle energies streaming from those higher octaves of being. The Great Work is not a poetic metaphor —it is a literal, scientific process of energetic descent and reception. And like any sacred exchange, there is a correct and formalized method for participating in this planetary alchemy.

This participation begins with a conscious, reverent relationship to the nervous system.

The nervous system is the subtle infrastructure of receptivity, the golden ladder linking the dense physical body to the invisible spiritual planes. As we come into deeper identification with its function and purification, we inevitably begin to feel the electromagnetic field it produces and maintains. This field is what has long been referred to as the aura.

In chemistry, the term auric is defined as "of gold, with a valence of three." This, too, is an occult hint. The human aura is a golden field—formed through the harmonious interplay of the three primary bodies of human energy: the mental, the astral (or emotional), and the causal (or soul body). Together, these form a trinity of force through which the monadic will may eventually express.

The aura becomes most radiant and clear when attention is first directed toward the purification and integration of the mental and astral bodies. These are the veils through which the soul-light must pass. As the mind becomes a still mirror and the emotions a calm sea, the causal body —the storehouse of soul wisdom and karmic identity— begins to radiate more fully through the field.

This radiation is not symbolic. It is literal and measurable. As the subtle vehicles evolve, the purified auric field becomes a fountain—an inexhaustible wellspring of higher energies cascading downward from the Solar Angel, passing through the causal body, and pouring outward into the world.

This is not fantasy. It is fact.

And soon, what the Initiates have long known will be verifiable by the outer sciences. As the instruments of measurement are refined—responding to the increasing vibration of humanity itself—this light field will be seen, mapped, and understood as a central phenomenon of consciousness. The sciences are catching up to the Ageless Wisdom, and the bridge is already under construction.

When we understand this, we realize: we are no longer waiting. We are becoming the very fulfillment of prophecy, the living vessels of the next revelation.

W.M.A.

Meditation for Radiant Alignment Through the Aura

Preparation:
Sit or lie down in a relaxed, supported position. Let the spine remain upright if possible, honoring it as the central channel of light. Allow your eyes to close and the breath to settle naturally.

Invocation (spoken inwardly or aloud):

"I align my physical, emotional, and mental bodies in preparation for the descent of Light."
"I call forth my Soul's presence into this sacred space."
"I dedicate this body, this field, and this moment to the Great Work."

Step 1: Nervous System Awareness
Bring your awareness to the base of the spine. Visualize a soft current of golden light beginning to rise gently upward, winding through your spinal column. This current is warm, steady, alive.

Follow it upward—vertebra by vertebra—until it reaches the brain, lighting up the neural pathways, illuminating the brainstem, the cerebrum, the pineal gland.

Now bring attention to the pituitary gland, just behind the center of the forehead. Feel it activate in response.

Let the pineal gland—surrounded by its crystalline structures—begin to pulse softly. Allow this pulse to extend gently outward, forming the inner magnetic spark of your auric field.

Step 2: Auric Expansion

Visualize your aura now as a golden-rose-white field expanding gently around you, about 3 to 6 feet in all directions. It is not static, but fluid—alive with light. It is composed of layered harmonics of your mental, emotional, and soul bodies.

As you inhale, see light pouring in from the crown. As you exhale, let it radiate outward through your aura, through your heart, into the world.

With every breath, the field strengthens and refines.

Step 3: Invocation of the Solar Angel

Now, silently call to the radiant Solar Angel—the higher presence watching over your journey through time.

You may say:

"Radiant Soul, Guardian Flame, I invite your presence."
"Shine through me. Guide me. Teach me."
"I am willing. I am ready. I am yours."

Pause here and simply listen. Feel the descending presence. It may arrive as a warmth, an image, a wordless knowing. Accept whatever comes.

Step 4: Completion and Sealing

Inhale deeply and envision a column of light descending from your monadic source—a pure stream of white fire above the crown. Let it meet your auric field and seal it in calm, clear protection.

Repeat inwardly:

"The work is done. I am aligned. I am radiant. I am whole."

Remain in silence for as long as needed.

A Moment of Raw, Human Tension
Uncollected Thoughts: Unedited Expression

After time, deep grief brings with it a golden layer of protective energy. It is through grief that we are given the greatest opportunity for the flowering of the hidden self—it is what casts the Light upon our innermost nature.

I carry him with me every single moment of every single day. To me, he is always present in my presence. I feel him guiding me—a palpable touch every now and again when I start to doubt that, or when my sorrow brings me to my knees.

For Him, time is mostly irrelevant. For Him, space is easily and rapidly traversed through the strength of Will alone. And despite how he went, he had a great and enjoyably witty sense of Will. My person has entered into the purest, most High embodiment of themselves.

I weep for my own sorrow—my own yearning for that most intimate touch—the touch of the Fiery World that met us as sparks flying down into us, from my mind to His, and vice versa. I weep for my own peace of mind: that which was lost from me, and to calibrate that which remains.

Everything is in a state of flux—even my vision of tomorrow is skewed and blurry and shifting. I'm not sure where my feet are taking me, or if they are even set in a definite direction. I am doing my best to allow the flow to take me, but currently, the direction of that flow is unpredictable and nerve-wracking. I've been crying a lot.

But it feels like my tears go nowhere. Even when I feel like you are listening and near, it feels like my tears go nowhere. I didn't know a human could cry so much, with so much sorrow. All I can do anymore is pray for Him to return—because I know when that happens, I will get to be with you again.

You were my heartbeat, my reason for breathing. You gave me a purpose and a love like I'd never known—or will ever know again. A writer, left in the world without his muse. It's terrible and ironic...to feel frozen and unable to tap into your power. Knowing that my power lies within the words I am able to transmit to others, yet feeling too overwhelmed and overstimulated to speak truth into the world.

What I'm terrified of most? Not knowing the amount of time I must wait to be with you again. There is no fear greater for me than that anymore. There is so much grief in me that I don't think there is room yet for anyone else.

It is a hard thing to learn to maintain strong boundaries and self-respect during the loneliest and most sorrowful time in my life. Maybe I just need to do—just do whatever it is that makes sense for me to immediately have what it is that I really want. Just do. There is no other option, really.

And I have ideas. And I have a partner to work with.

A different mountain range, but I am still here—alive and breathing...sad but hopeful, sad but not surprised. I have everything I need out here. I don't know if I'll ever go back. I know I can never go back to the way things were, and it is divinely guided that I am not at home for now, so

I can find my true Home—which is on the Earth, wherever I may find myself.

Inspiration is returning to me, and I've only been here for one night and one day. My ears are filled with music for now. It's helping me to find security in my surroundings so that I cannot hear other people speaking clearly, and that helps me think more clearly. When I can hear voices, I feel the energy they carry, and my shields are weak for now. They will begin truly repairing themselves the longer I am surrounded by the Mother's incredible manifestations.

It is still hard for me to see through the glamour that echoes from the hearts of other people, especially young people who are completely consumed by their egos still... oh, the ignorance of some youth... It's not a bad thing— we all go through it to some extent.

For now, the sound of the stream, the breeze, the trees— they are distraction enough from the remaining loudness that people bring with them wherever they seem to go. I am only at this campground because fate took me here, and I am seeing the beauty in the situation—grateful for the reassurance and assistance from people who are genuinely kind and compassionate. I think those are the type of people I am bound to meet on my adventures, and for the most part, I am open to receiving them. It is going to take work to continue to open up and lose the intrusive thoughts that people are actively judging me. We are all judging each other all the time, and so it is completely irrelevant.

First of all, I am meant to trigger people, and I always have—so I mostly have removed personality from the equation, which provides for the relinquishment of the burden of the impressions of others. Minding my own business and focusing on sharing my wisdom with you, dear reader. These trees are helping to electrify my mind —to write without the impediments of the city.

The magnetism of the Earth is so strong here, where there are not thousands of EMF sources screeching through the fabric of reality. In the quiet, with only the sounds of the animals, the trees whisper to my spirit—connecting me like an antenna to the greatness of the Life of the Earth. As this connection strengthens, my body is beginning to release all excess energy that no longer serves it. The Mother is glad to receive these energies; no human thing is too great for the Mother to transmute.

The real Power becomes something palpable, even understandable to some extent. The waves of it begin to enter into and heal this broken mind and weary body.

Although the sorrow of grief follows in every footstep on the Way, it is becoming quite clear that the world we dreamed up together is becoming the reality currently unfolding on the planet. He would be both greatly disturbed and deeply hopeful because of the events that have occurred since his passing. If it has not become clear yet, I write for the memory of Him—my Twin Flame, the Fire in my Heart.

In this year of 2024, great things have occurred in rapid succession in such a way that most people have had no real, deep perception of them. The old World is crumbling and dying to make way for the New World and the awesome discovery of the reality of the Soul and its Great

Purpose. Humanity is quickly stumbling toward the realization of Infinity and the incredible implications that will stream forth because of that momentous discovery.

Once the Soul becomes a subject of tangible research and scientific exploration, new and great heights will be possible—and humanity will begin to comprehend the extent of their personal power, and how that coalesces with (and empowers or degrades) the Group Soul and the purpose it serves. Many ranking members of Hierarchy who descend to Earth naturally return to even more profound work when they arrive back into the higher realms after passing out of their earthly incarnation.

"I didn't mind it... because I knew that it takes getting everything you ever wanted, and then losing it, to find true freedom." –LDR

Throughout my entire youth and young adulthood, I wished for a love that was real, deep, raw, and honest. I found that—and for seven years, was given the gift of being loved and held up by the most brilliant, most beautiful human being to have walked this planet. He brought me to life and saved me from myself on countless occasions.

Unfortunately, his time came far too soon, and here I sit, learning how to be without him. My one reprieve is writing for you, dear friend, so that you know that you are not alone in the struggles, sorrow, and grief that you carry with you every day. I am with you—and so are they.

I have discussed in the past the incredible importance of the process of alignment. This is critical: alignment with one's life circumstance, alignment with the most evolved parts of the physical and emotional self, and ultimately, alignment with the Solar Angel, or the Light of one's own Soul. Through this alignment, we may achieve the state of consciousness required to operate as a Group Soul on the mental plane. This is where the most effective Work can take place—where the New Group of World Servers are changing the world and drawing Light down to meet the need of the time.

It is here, on the mental plane, that we may work directly with the energy being sent forth into humanity from the Hierarchy. This energy can only be utilized through the active Will of humanity—and this is because the Hierarchy, by law, cannot directly interfere in the course of human endeavor and evolution unless we reach out and ask them for assistance. When we draw ourselves close to the Master and take our places in the outer ashrams, sitting with our backs to the Temple of Light and streaming that Light forth into humanity through the activity of the seven major centers in the body—

This is how we change the course of human affairs. And there are enough of us here Now to enact that change, if we take the right action and reach out for the Light. It is time to remember the truth of your identity, my friend. It is time to open your eyes to the bigger picture—and you may zoom out and make that picture as big as you'd like. That is the profound nature of Infinity, and of Consciousness. I have nothing but pure belief in your ability to find your way back Home to your Self.

I have tried to flee from it, from all of it, many times—and have found the same result each time: a reorientation right back to where I began. Sometimes the next step, after the final step, makes it feel like being taken backwards—but this is not so. The Law prevents us from ever moving backwards. It is just a new way—the beginning of the next chapter, the Journey of the Fool stumbling gratefully into the beginning of his next great adventure.

As the days continue to pass, the Way becomes more clear for those who see through the Maya and peer into the inner world of meaning. The Age of Aquarius is rapidly replacing the old principles of the Age of Pisces and the zealous devotion of the major world religions that blossomed during that age.

Aligning oneself with Divine Will brings forth an unimpeded stream of Pure Reason into the individual's consciousness. In this state, it becomes easily recognizable how the tapestry of reality—including its varied stories and illusions—is interwoven with the subtle realms layered upon and within it.

Falling in and out of Divine Will is part of the process, but know that every time it is achieved—even if for a moment—it becomes more familiar, more attainable, and thus sustainable for longer periods.

For as complex as the Plan may feel, it may be simplified in a single word: kindness. Acts of kindness toward one's fellow beings in all kingdoms of nature culminate in the unfolding of the Divine Plan on Earth. Kindness is not subjective—and the roots of understanding altruistic and pure kindness may be found in the mannerisms and unconditional love shown by small children, animals, and the inherently supportive nature of the plant kingdom.

Cultivating kindness toward the Self and toward one's own body and mind—this is the most profound place to begin. You embody a universe, and acts of kindness toward the Self echo into what is the microcosm of your macrocosmic identity. Here lies a simple path toward calibrating accumulated karmic imbalance. Your life is not only your own. It belongs to a multitude of smaller lives within your being. If you are able to cognize this in a way that allows you to reflect the understanding into the Greater Lives we exist within, it will help you to understand the nature of Reality and Infinity just a little bit better.

Subtle teaching through the wisdom of the Light of the Soul—without frustration or judgment—is the only reasonable way forward into developing humanity's collective access to the Infinity of Consciousness. Frustration adds to the state of disharmony already so prevalent in societies across the globe, especially during this time of great flux. It deepens the problem of division and separateness for one to place themselves on a pedestal and call themselves anything other than a fellow seeker, a fellow student.

There is power in leveling with others, regardless of your assumption of their intellectual prowess. A true seeker on the Way always perceives first through the lens of heart-centered consciousness. This aligns the mind with a state of Pure Reason, whose nature it is to dissolve any remaining sense of separateness from one's fellows. The fallacy of division between the *You* and *I* must be overcome first—before the New World Order can even begin to fully sink its roots beneath our wandering feet. When it does, any of us who are even beginning to wipe the sleep from our eyes will have the same dawning of awareness:

We do not walk alone.

That is what will first be realized—and that realization, in and of itself, will have a profound impact on the journey of humanity itself. The unseen worlds will begin to exist in our fields of awareness, and those higher Beings, including the Masters, will be seen walking amongst the world of humanity.

"I'm missing you, and all the things we used to do."

It is through the grief of the *loss* of the independent reflection of myself that I have awakened to the fabric between the lands of the unseen worlds—and I traverse them now at will. And through that awakening, his presence has become something tangible and accessible to me even as I walk through the mundane.

At the edge of life and death, I found myself clinging to the idea of moving on from this life willingly. Fortunately, it is not up to one to decide when or how that great transition occurs—not without karmic balancing beyond the veil. The knowing fueled me to choose to keep walking forward, attempting to fulfill the purpose that only his infinite love for me fuels me to continue working toward.

And so the journey continues...

We shall meet again soon, my dear friend. In Lighted Companionship,

W.M.A.

Glossary of Esoteric Terms

This glossary is intended to aid readers new to the Ageless Wisdom tradition. Definitions are simplified for clarity while retaining the essential occult meanings.

Agni Yoga – A path of fiery, heart-centered spiritual practice that synthesizes action, intuition, and higher consciousness. Named after Agni, the fire of divine will.

Ashram – A spiritual group or center under the guidance of a Master of Wisdom, existing on the mental plane and linked to the Hierarchy.

Aura – The energetic field surrounding all living beings. Composed of several layers reflecting physical vitality, emotions, thoughts, and spiritual states.

Causal Body – The vehicle of the Soul on the higher mental plane; the storehouse of all accumulated wisdom from incarnations.

Deva – A being of the angelic evolution; devas are builders of form and work with the energies of nature and creation.

Disciple – One who has committed to the path of spiritual service, often under the guidance of a Master.

Dweller on the Threshold – The sum total of unresolved karma, fear, and lower impulses that confront the disciple before initiation.

Etheric Body – The subtle energy blueprint of the physical body through which life force (prana) flows.

Glamour – Emotional and mental illusion that distorts spiritual truth, particularly prevalent on the astral plane.

Hierarchy (Planetary) – The inner government of the world composed of Masters of Wisdom and divine beings guiding the evolution of humanity.

Initiation – A stage of conscious spiritual advancement, marked by expanded awareness and increased capacity for service. Governed by the Hierarchy.

Karma – The law of cause and effect governing all actions and their consequences across lifetimes.

Logos – A divine being or intelligence governing a planetary, solar, or cosmic system. The Solar Logos is the deity of our solar system.

Monad – The pure spiritual essence at the core of every being; the true Self beyond the Soul.

Personality – The temporary vehicle for the Soul, composed of the physical, astral (emotional), and mental bodies.

Ray – A stream of divine energy with specific qualities and purposes. Seven major Rays govern both the universe and the individual psyche.

Sanat Kumara – The Lord of the World and regent of the Planetary Logos. He embodies divine purpose and anchors Shamballa on Earth.

Shamballa – The planetary spiritual center where the will of God is known. The dwelling of Sanat Kumara and the central point of divine government.

Solar Angel – The higher aspect of the Soul that acts as a guide and builder of the causal body; a radiant intermediary between the Monad and the lower self.

Soul – The immortal, conscious identity that evolves through lifetimes. The mediating principle between Spirit and matter.

Triad (Spiritual Triad) – The higher triplicity of atma (spiritual will), buddhi (intuition), and manas (higher mind) which reflects the Monad.

White Magic – The science of right spiritual creation and manifestation, practiced harmlessly and in service to the Plan.

Suggested Reading & Foundational Works of the Ageless Wisdom

This text is the result of a personal journey into the living light of truth, and it would not exist without the guidance and influence of the great spiritual teachers and texts that came before it. For those who wish to continue their study and deepen their understanding, the following works are highly recommended:

Helena Petrovna Blavatsky

- *The Secret Doctrine* (Vols. I & II)

- *The Voice of the Silence*

- *Isis Unveiled*

Alice A. Bailey (with the Tibetan Master Djwhal Khul)

- *Initiation: Human and Solar*

- *A Treatise on White Magic*

- *A Treatise on Cosmic Fire*

- *Discipleship in the New Age* (Vols. I & II)

- *The Rays and the Initiations*

- *From Intellect to Intuition*

- *Glamour: A World Problem*

- *The Externalisation of the Hierarchy*

- *The Reappearance of the Christ*

Agni Yoga Society

- *Agni Yoga*

- *Leaves of Morya's Garden* (Books I & II)

- *Heart*

- *Supermundane* (Volumes I–IV)

Lucille Cedercrans

- *The Nature of the Soul*

- *Creative Thinking*

- *The Disciple and Economy*

Manly P. Hall

- *The Secret Teachings of All Ages*

Dion Fortune

- *The Mystical Qabalah*

- *The Cosmic Doctrine*

Sri Aurobindo & The Mother

- *The Life Divine*

- *Letters on Yoga*

Additional Key Influences

- *The Bhagavad Gita* (translated with esoteric commentary)

- *The Upanishads*

- *The Tao Te Ching* (Laozi)

- *The Corpus Hermeticum* (Hermes Trismegistus)

About the Author

Wyatt Ambrose is a spiritual writer, seeker, and channel for the Fire of the Soul. Having walked the path of suffering, initiation, and revelation, he offers his work as a living record of personal transformation and esoteric service. Guided by a deep inner knowing, his teachings reflect the Ageless Wisdom tradition while remaining rooted in the immediacy of lived experience. Wyatt writes not to preach, but to accompany fellow travelers on the Way. This book is both a love letter to humanity and a transmission of Light—crafted in the silent companionship of his Higher Self and in sacred memory of a love that endures beyond the veil.

Made in the USA
Monee, IL
11 May 2025

17247829R00187